The SELECTION and ELECTION of PRESIDENTS

The **SELECTION** and **ELECTION** of **PRESIDENTS**

ROBERT S. HIRSCHFIELD
editor

ALDINETRANSACTION
A Division of Transaction Publishers
New Brunswick (U.S.A.) and London (U.K.)

Copyright © 2009 by Transaction Publishers, New Brunswick, New Jersey.

All rights reserved under International and Pan-American Copyright Conventions. No part of this book may be reproduced or transmitted in any form or by any means, electronic or mechanical, including photocopy, recording, or any information storage and retrieval system, without prior permission in writing from the publisher. All inquiries should be addressed to AldineTransaction, A Division of Transaction Publishers, Rutgers—The State University, 35 Berrue Circle, Piscataway, New Jersey 08854-8042. www.transactionpub.com

This book is printed on acid-free paper that meets the American National Standard for Permanence of Paper for Printed Library Materials.

Library of Congress Catalog Number: 2008055027
ISBN: 978-0-202-36276-2
Printed in the United States of America

Library of Congress Cataloging-in-Publication Data

Selection/election.
  The selection and election of presidents / [edited by] Robert S. Hirschfield.
      p. cm.
  Papers from a two-week seminar organized by the French-American Foundation and held in 1980.
    Originally published: Selection/election. New York : Aldine Pub. Co., 1982.
  Includes bibliographical references and index.
  ISBN 978-0-202-36276-2 (alk. paper)
     1. Presidents—United States—Election—Congresses. I. Hirschfield, Robert S. II. French-American Foundation. III. Title.

JK524.S47   2009
324.60973—dc22
                                                                                         2008055027

Contents

The Editor	vii
The Contributors	ix
Preface *Arthur King Peters*	xvii
Introduction: Reforming the Reforms *Robert S. Hirschfield*	xxi

I. Understanding Presidential Politics
    Jeane J. Kirkpatrick
    Austin Ranney
    Howard R. Penniman
    Norman J. Ornstein
    Thomas E. Mann
	1

II. The Electoral System:
Voters, Parties, Candidates
    Richard M. Scammon
    Carol Bellamy
	21

III. The Electoral System: Media and Money
    Edward N. Costikyan
    John W. McGarry
	37

IV. The Nominating Process:
Primaries and Delegate Selection
    Gerald M. Pomper
    Miriam Bockman
	51

V.	The Nominating Process: Conventions *Rita W. Cooley* *Basil A. Paterson*	71
VI.	Presidential Campaigns: Strategies and Tactics *Richard M. Pious* *Robert C. Weaver*	89
VII.	Presidential Campaigns: Press, Polls, Packaging *Douglas Ireland* *Murray Edelman*	107
VIII.	Is This Any Way to Elect a President? *Eugene J. McCarthy* *Shirley Chisholm* *James Q. Wilson* *Steven Brams*	117
Questions and Comments on the Selection/ Election Process		141

The Editor

Robert S. Hirschfield is Professor and Chairman of the Department of Political Science at Hunter College/City University of New York. He received his Ph.D. from New York University and his A.B., LL.B., and M. A. from Harvard University. Author of THE CONSTITUTION AND THE COURT and editor of THE POWER OF THE PRESIDENCY, now in its third edition, his articles, essays, and reviews have appeared in *Public Policy, Parliamentary Affairs, The American Political Science Review, The American Government Annual, The Nation, the New York Times,* and other journals. He has taught at Harvard, Fordham, and New York University. Dr. Hirschfield is Director of the New York Center for Education in Politics, and has been a political activist at both the national and local levels. He is also the producer and host of a public affairs television program in New York City.

Contributors

CAROL BELLAMY is President of the New York City Council—the second highest post in City government. She is the first woman elected to city-wide office in New York. As Council President Ms. Bellamy is also New York's Ombudsman. Ms. Bellamy grew up in Plainfield, New Jersey. After graduating from Gettysburg College in Pennsylvania, she served two years with the Peace Corps in Guatemala. She then entered New York University Law School, was admitted to the New York Bar in 1968, and joined the Wall Street firm of Cravath, Swaine and Moore. Elected to the State Senate in 1972, she served as ranking Democrat on the Cities Committee and chaired the Senate Democratic Task Force on the City of New York.

MIRIAM BOCKMAN was until 1981 Leader of the New York County Democratic Committee (formerly Tammany Hall). She is First Vice-Chair of the New York State Democratic Committee, and was Vice Chair of the New York State Delegation to the 1981 Democratic National Convention. The first woman to be County Leader in New York City, Ms. Bockman has been Democratic District Leader in the Greenwich Village area since 1969. She is closely associated with the reform movement in the Democratic Party, and has been deeply concerned with women's rights, urban and health issues. She is a member of the New York City Commission on the Status of Women and has been a member of her local Community Board since 1970. She is a graduate of Hunter College.

STEVEN J. BRAMS is Professor of Politics at New York University. He received his B.S. from Massachusetts Institute of Technology and his Ph.D. from Northwestern University. He is the author of

Game Theory and Politics, Paradoxes in Politics, The Presidential Election Game, and *Biblical Games: A Strategic Analysis of Stories in the Old Testament.* He is a member of the editorial boards of the *American Political Science Review* and the *Journal of Politics.*

SHIRLEY CHISHOLM represents the 12th District of New York (Brooklyn) in the United States House of Representatives. Educated at Brooklyn College (B.A.) and Columbia University (M.A.) she was a teacher and directed a nursery school until her election to the New York State Assembly in 1964. She has received awards for work in child welfare and her legislative achievements from the NAACP and other organizations. She is the author of *Unbought and Unbossed* and *The Good Fight.* In 1972 Mrs. Chisholm was a candidate for President of the United States.

RITA W. COOLEY is Professor of Politics at New York University. She was educated at Hunter College and New York University. Dr. Cooley is a winner of six "Golden Dozen" Awards from New York University undergraduates who vote annually on the twelve teachers who contributed most to their education. She also won the 1967 "Great Teacher Award" at New York University, and she was elected to the Hunter College Hall of Fame in 1970. She was Director of the Citizenship Clearing House for Southern New York, 1952-1957. Her publications include a textbook on American Government and a number of articles on teaching political science.

EDWARD N. COSTIKYAN was born in Weehawken, New Jersey, and educated at Columbia University. He was admitted to the bar in 1949 and is at present a partner in the law firm of Paul, Weiss, Rifkind, Wharton and Garrison. Mr. Costikyan entered politics at the encouragement of Adlai Stevenson, whose law partner he later became. In 1955 he was elected a Democratic district leader and later became head of "Tammany Hall" (the New York County Democratic Committee). He has been a major figure in the New York Reform Democratic movement, helped frame the city's newly revised Charter, and in 1977 was a candidate for the Democratic nomination for mayor. His book, *Behind Closed Doors,* is a study of the "old" politics and is used as a text in many political science courses. His latest work, *How To Win Votes: The Politics of 1980* is about the "new" politics and the campaign strategies it dictates.

MURRAY EDELMAN has worked for CBS News since 1967 and is currently Associate Director of its Election Survey Unit. He supervises the CBS/New York Times surveys, and is responsible for sample design, data collection and analysis for CBS election programs. He has participated in calling over 600 races—with only one error. Mr. Edelman received his Ph.D. from the University of Chicago and his B.A. from the University of Illinois. His articles have appeared in Social Science Information and he has contributed to books on the development of attention structure in children.

DOUGLAS IRELAND, a former *New York Post* reporter, has written for the *Village Voice, The Nation, Dissent, The New York Times Sunday Magazine,* and *The Washington Post.* In 1977 he headed an investigative team that covered the Bert Lance affair for *New York Magazine.* He writes a political column for the *Soho News,* and is at work on a novel about New York City politics. Mr. Ireland's activities in electoral politics include coordinating the six-state Mid-Atlantic Region in Eugene McCarthy's 1968 presidential campaign; managing Bella Abzug's first successful race for Congress in 1970 and her losing race for the U.S. Senate against Daniel Patrick Moynihan in 1976; and running Paul O'Dwyer's successful campaign for City Council President in 1973.

JEANE J. KIRKPATRICK was appointed Chief United States Representative to the United Nations by President Reagan in January 1981. Prior to that, she was University Professor at Georgetown University and a Resident Scholar at the American Enterprise Institute for Public Policy Research. Dr. Kirkpatrick took her A.B. at Barnard College and her M.A. and Ph.D. at Columbia University. She was a French Government Fellow at the Institute of Political Science of the University of Paris and has lectured in France at the University of Aix-Marseilles and Aix-en-Provence under the auspices of the Institute for American Universities. She is the author of *The New Presidential Elite, Political Woman, Leader and Vanguard in Mass Society: A Study of Peronist Argentina, Dismantling the Parties: Reflections on Party Reform and Party Decomposition,* and *On the Celebration of Hubert Humphrey* (forthcoming).

THOMAS E. MANN became Executive Director of the American Political Science Association in 1981. He has been a political polling consultant and a member of the Democratic National Committee's Commission on Presidential Nomination and Party Structure. Educated at the University of Florida (B.A.) and the University of Michigan (M.A. and Ph.D.), Dr. Mann was an APSA Congressional Fellow and served as legislative assistant to Representative James O'Hara (D-Michigan) and Senator Philip A. Hart (D-Michigan). He is the author of *Unsafe At Any Margin: Interpreting Congressional Elections* and *Career Alternatives for Political Scientists: A Guide for Faculty and Graduate Students.*

EUGENE J. MCCARTHY was United States Senator from Minnesota from 1958 to 1970. He was a candidate for President in 1968 and 1972. Educated at St. John's University (Minnesota) and the University of Minnesota he taught economics and sociology before being elected to the U.S. House of Representatives in 1946. Senator McCarthy served as Adlai Stevenson Professor of Political Science at the New School for Social Research in 1973-1974 and has been a syndicated columnist since 1977. He is the author of *Frontiers In American Democracy, Dictionary of American Politics, A Liberal Answer to the Conservative Challenge, The Limits of Power, The Year of the People, America Revisited,* and a book of poetry.

JOHN WARREN McGARRY is a native of Massachusetts. He was appointed to the Federal Election Commission in 1978 by President Carter, and was named Vice Chairman in 1980. Commissioner McGarry graduated cum laude from Holy Cross College in Massachusetts in 1952. He subsequently did graduate work at Boston University and obtained a Juris Doctor degree from Georgetown Law Center in 1956. From 1959 through 1962, Mr. McGarry was Assistant Attorney General of Massachusetts. He then combined private law practice with service as Chief Counsel for the Special Committee to Investigate Campaign Expenditures of the U.S.

House of Representatives. From 1973 until his appointment to the Election Commission, Mr. McGarry served as Special Counsel on Elections to the Committee on House Administration of the U.S. Congress.

NORMAN J. ORNSTEIN received his B.A. from the University of Minnesota; his M.A. and Ph.D. from the University of Michigan. He has taught political science at Eastern Michigan University and Johns Hopkins University. He is now Associate Professor at the Catholic University of America. Professor Ornstein has served as Staff Assistant to Congressman Donald M. Fraser (D-Minnesota) and to Senator George McGovern (D-South Dakota). He has also been a consultant for the National Opinion Research Center and the Commission on the Operation of the Senate. He is the editor of *Congress in Change: Evolution and Reform,* and *Interest Groups, Lobbying and Policymaking.*

BASIL A. PATERSON was named Secretary of State of New York in 1979. Before that he served in the New York State Senate, was the Democratic candidate for Lt. Governor in 1970, and was Vice Chairman of the Democratic National Committee from 1972 to 1977. He is also President of the New York City branch of the NAACP. Mr. Paterson attended New York City public schools and graduated from DeWitt Clinton High School. He received a Bachelor of Science degree from St. John's College and a Juris Doctorate from St. John's Law School. He has been a visiting professor at State University at New Paltz, an adjunct professor at Fordham University School of Education and a visiting professor at City University of New York.

HOWARD R. PENNIMAN received his B.A. and M.A. from Louisiana State University, and his Ph.D. from the University of Minnesota. He has taught at the University of Alabama, Yale, and Georgetown University. He is an Adjunct Scholar at the American Enterprise Institute for Public Policy Research and election consultant for the American Broadcasting Company. Professor Penniman is the author of *Government and Politics in the United*

States, *The American Political Process, Elections in South Vietnam, Campaign Finances: Two Views of the Political and Constitutional Implications,* and editor of *France at the Polls: The Presidential Election of 1974.*

RICHARD M. PIOUS is the author of *The American Presidency* and of *Civil Rights and Liberties in the 1970's.* He has edited a ten-volume series in public law and the forthcoming Centennial Proceedings of the Academy of Political Science (New York). Dr. Pious teaches at Barnard College and is a member of the graduate faculty at Columbia University. A participant in the Columbia School of Journalism 1980 Institute for Presidential Coverage, Dr. Pious served as a presidential campaign consultant in 1976 and 1980.

GERALD M. POMPER is Professor and Chairman of the Political Science Department at Rutgers, the State University of New Jersey, and Director of the Center on Political Parties at its Eagleton Institute. He received his B.A. from Columbia and his Ph.D. from Princeton. He taught at City College/ City University of New York for three years before going to Rutgers in 1962 and has been there since, except for a Fulbright year in Israel. His publications include ten books, including *Nominating the President, Elections in America, The Election of 1976, Voters' Choice* and *American Party Renewal.*

AUSTIN RANNEY has served a President of the American Political Science Association and as Managing Editor of the *American Political Science Review.* He was educated at Northwestern University (B.S.), the University of Oregon (M. A.), and Yale University (Ph.D.). He has taught at Yale, the University of Illinois, and the University of Wisconsin/ Madison. Since 1976 he has been a Resident Scholar at the American Enterprise Institute for Public Policy Research. Dr. Ranney has served as a member of Democratic National Committee's Commission on Presidential Nomination and Party Structure. His publications include *The Federalization of Presidential Primaries, Participation in American Presidential*

Nominations, Curing the Mischiefs of Faction: Party Reforms in America, Pathways to Parliament, Illinois Politics, The Governing of Men, Democracy and the American Party System (with Willmore Kendall), and *The Doctrine of Responsible Party Government.*

RICHARD M. SCAMMON is a native of Minneapolis, Minnesota. He was educated at the universities of Minnesota and Michigan, and at the London School of Economics. Since 1955 he has been Director of the Elections Research Center in Washington, D.C., except for 1961-65 when he took leave to serve as Director of the U.S. Bureau of the Census. Elections consultant for NBC News, Mr. Scammon has also lectured at Howard, Johns Hopkins, George Washington and York (Ontario) universities; and for the U.S. International Communication Agency. He is Editor of *America at the Polls* (1965) and of the *American Votes* series (1956-1979). He has also co-authored *This U.S.A.* (1965) and *The Real Majority* (1970).

ROBERT C. WEAVER became the first black person appointed to a Presidential Cabinet when he was appointed Secretary of Housing and Urban Development by President Johnson in 1966. Educated at Harvard University (B.S., M.S., Ph.D.), Professor Weaver has taught at Columbia University and Hunter College. He has held a number of positions in government at the city and state as well as at the federal level. He is a former chairman of the NAACP, and is the author of *Negro Labor, The Negro Ghetto, The Urban Complex,* and *Dilemmas of Urban America.*

JAMES Q. WILSON has taught since 1961 at Harvard University, where he is now the Henry Lee Shattuck Professor of Government. Raised in California, Mr. Wilson attended the University of Redlands and received his Ph.D. from the University of Chicago. While at Harvard, he has been chairman of the Department of Government, director of the Joint Center for Urban Studies of MIT and Harvard, and chairman of a task force whose report led to the creation of the Core Curriculum. He has also served in a number of advisory posts in the federal government, and is a Fellow of the

American Academy of Arts and Sciences. Professor Wilson is the author of *American Government and Institutions, Negro Politics, The Amateur Democrat, City Politics* (with Edward C. Banfield), *Varieties of Police Behavior, Political Organizations, Thinking About Crime,* and *The Investigators.* now in its third edition, his articles, essays, and reviews have appeared in *Public Policy, Parliamentary Affairs, The American Political Science Review, The American Government Annual, The Nation, the New York Times,* and other journals. He has taught at Harvard, Fordham, and New York University. Dr. Hirschfield is Director of the New York Center for Education in Politics, and has been a political activist at both the national and local levels. He is also the producer and host of a public affairs television program in New York City.

Preface

The American Political Process: Election 1980 was a two week seminar organized by the French-American Foundation to show future French leaders how Americans select their president.

Our presidential selection process, which is intricate, constantly evolving, and imperfectly understood even by most American voters, is too often described by the French press in simplistic and outmoded terms that confuse rather than clarify. The French-American Foundation viewed the 1980 presidential campaign as offering special opportunities to offset some of these misperceptions. Through our program, French political specialists could witness the intense self-scrutiny which occurs every four years during the American presidential election campaign. At no other time are the complex political structures, personalities, and socio-economic forces that shape the presidential selection process so clearly visible as in the months leading to a national election. The long campaign brings to light conflicting concepts of the role of the President, inherent constraints on his powers, contradictions in the selection process, and the possibilities for change or compromise which are at once its strength and its weakness. As it turned out, project participants also watched presidential power pass from one political party to another—as they were to do in France in 1981.

The French-American Foundation, from its vantage point as a non-political and nonpartisan organization, selected twenty candidates, age 25 to 37, as seminar participants after interviews in Paris by the Foundation staff. The group of French professionals from government, media, universities, law, business and industry, labor unions and political parties was joined by representatives from West Germany, Belgium, Spain, and Monaco. Each participant had a career interest in observing the American political scene. Most professed, at the conclusion of the seminar that it had been a formative experience which profoundly modified their views of the American presidency as well as the selection process. A number of participants also indicated that the American experience stimulated them to rethink certain aspects of the French electoral system. The 1981 French presidential and assembly elections will no doubt provoke further comparisons and analysis by these participants for some time to come.

The program had four main components: 1) an opening orientation weekend featuring keynote speakers; 2) meetings in New York City with presentations by academic authorities on the presidency, party and elected officials, political analysts and campaign consultants; 3) on-site visits in Washington and Detroit; and 4) a closing panel discussion and dinner with two former presidential candidates participating.

In Washington the project members were briefed at the White House by Ambassador Alonzo McDonald, Staff Director for the President, on Capitol Hill and at the French Embassy by Francois de Laboulaye, Ambassador of France. Sargent Shriver, former United States Ambassador to France, interpreted Convention activities, and a news briefing was held at the *Washington Post.* Professor Jeane Kirkpatrick, now United States Ambassador to the United Nations, chaired a panel discussion at the American Enterprise Institute. In Detroit, the participants attended part of the Republican National Convention, where they were addressed by Richard Allen, now Assistant to the President for National Security Affairs.

The program, judging from the evaluations of all concerned, succeeded in accomplishing its objectives: to draw for the participants an accurate picture of how the President of the United States is selected, to analyze central aspects and problems of the selection/election process, and to elicit discussion of possible improvements in that system.

The French-American Foundation, which in 1981 celebrates its fifth anniversary, is a nonprofit, operating foundation whose purpose is to strengthen relations between the United States and France. The current Foundation program focuses on projects in communications and education which create new working relationships between young French and American professionals, future leaders involved with problems of major concern in both societies. A basic goal of Foundation activities is to keep each country's view of the other up-to-date and to reduce misperceptions that impede mutual understanding.

The annual series of Seminars in Contemporary American Studies for young French professionals is one of many projects organized by the Foundation in keeping with this fundamental purpose. A committee of Foundation directors, under the chairmanship of James Chace, managing editor of *Foreign Affairs,* oversees the planning of each seminar. In 1979, the seminar considered "The United States in the World Economy" and in 1981, in association with the Aspen Institute of Humanistic Studies, the subject for examination is "U.S. Television News."

In organizing and conducting our 1980 seminar on the American presidential selection process, the Foundation was fortunate to have Professor Robert Hirschfield, Chairman of the Political Science Department at Hunter College/City University of New York as Project Director. We are deeply indebted to him and to the remarkable roster of lecturers and panelists he assembled across a wide spectrum of political and professional backgrounds. Together with Constance C. Jewitt, Executive Director of the French-American Foundation, they assured the success of what the French participants found to be a truly enlightening experience. The French-American Foundation is also indebted to Exxon Education Foundation, the German Marshall Fund of the United States and Mobil Oil Corporation for their generous seminar grants, and to Mr. Guy Charlap, Mrs. Elizabeth Fondaras, and Ambassadors Francois de Laboulaye, Alonzo McDonald and Sargent Shriver; the American Enterprise Institute, Atlantik Br'ucke, Commission for Educational Exchange (Belgium), Ford Motor Company, Institute of French Studies (NYU), Museum of Broadcasting, International Communication Agency and the *Washington Post,* for their special contributions.

Arthur King Peters, Chairman
French-American Foundation
New York

Introduction

The heart of the French-American Foundation's project *The American Political Process: Election 1980* was a series of meetings and seminars dealing with the presidential selection/election process.

A varied group of practitioners and professional students of American government and politics made presentations at these sessions. The guest speakers ranged from former presidential candidates to party leaders to professors. The setting was informal, there was much give and take between the speakers, and questions from the project participants.

Each of the seminars was designed to focus on a particular element in the selection/election system—parties, for example—to describe its operation, to analyze its relationship to the other elements, and to assess its efficacy in the light of recent changes or "reforms." Inevitably, the seminar sessions, like the general meetings, ended up discussing and assessing the entire system.

In all, nine sessions were held. Taken together they constituted an expert critique of the political process as it moved toward the choice of a President in 1980. What emerged from the two week forum was a remarkable consensus that the "new politics" in America has created as many problems as it has solved, that there is an urgent need to review the changes which have taken place in the political system during the past decade or so, and that to make the system work better we must "reform the reforms."

This agreement on the need for systemic revision included politicians and academicians alike and encompassed every important aspect of the selection/election process. Virtually every speaker, for example, agreed that the decline of the two major parties had destabilized the political system and created a situation potentially dangerous to the future of effective government in America. It was noted repeatedly that the important roles once played by the parties have changed radically over the past dozen years. These changes were the result of reforms which took place first and mainly in the Democratic Party after its turbulent 1968 convention. Long debated and finally achieved in response to the revolutionary atmosphere created by the anti-Vietnam movement, the reforms were designed to broaden the base of party participation and to democratize party decision-making. The rules regarding the party's key functions of selecting and electing a presidential candidate were changed to assure adequate representation of women and minority members at the party's national convention, to guarantee a fair reflection of each state's support for all potential candidates, and to encourage greater citizen participation in the selection of convention delegates through state presidential primaries.

Coincident with these changes in party rules, a new federal election law, passed in response to the Watergate scandal, attempted to reform the campaign financing system. Under this 1974 act a presidential candidate is given the choice of accepting or foregoing public financing of his campaign. If the candidate chooses the former method and raises $5,000 in each of at least 20 states through contributions of $250 or less, he qualifies for (and is limited to) $10 million for the primary campaign. Individual contributions to a primary candidate are limited to $1,000; political action committees may give $5,000. The major candidates in the general election are funded according to a formula established by the Federal Election Commission. In 1980 Jimmy Carter and Ronald Reagan each received $29.4 million; John Anderson finally received $4.2 million.

The combination of public financing and party-democratizing reforms has had profound effects on the selection/election system. Democratization, for example, led to a rapid proliferation of state primaries and a dramatic increase in the number of national convention delegates elected in such primaries. In 1968 the Democrats selected 40 percent of their delegates in 17 state primaries; in 1980 they selected 80 percent in 34 primaries. Although starting later, the Republicans by 1980 selected 76 percent of their delegates in

35 primaries. These delegates are not free to exercise independent judgment, however, since under most state laws they are pledged to vote on the first ballot for the candidate they supported in the primary. Finally, convention delegations are now almost devoid of party officials or office holders because such people are reluctant to commit themselves to a single candidate or to run for election as delegates. In short, the conventions now function merely to ratify the primary results, not to make professional political determinations or to find a broadly acceptable candidate for the party and the nation.

With public financing added to democratization, still more of the side effects of reformism become apparent. Such changes include: extending the length of campaigns, increasing the number and ideological range of candidates, involving more single-interest groups directly in the election process, and encouraging candidacies by those who are "outside" the governmental system.

The selection/election process can take as long as two years. Jimmy Carter—the first President elected under the new rules—actually announced his formal candidacy 19 months before the 1976 Democratic Convention. After his abortive try for the nomination at the Republican Convention in that same year, Ronald Reagan stopped only for a short breathing spell before beginning his 1980 campaign. Candidates must now be willing and able to make a long-range, full-time commitment to organize at the grass-roots level in virtually every state; to prepare for a plethora of local and state caucuses, conventions, and primaries; and to raise the money they need either for private funding or to qualify for public campaign financing.

The availability of public money induces and the primary election method encourages more narrowly based candidates to run, since successful fund raising and electoral appeals can be focused on special or even single-interest groups. And, given the amount of time and energy that must be spent in all these activities, the advantage lies with those who do not have continuing responsibilities in the public or private sectors. It is not surprising that Mr. Carter and Mr. Reagan were both ex-Governors and "unemployed" at the time of their campaigns for the presidency.

The "outsider" factor in campaigning also joins with the absence of selection input by party professionals to create a serious potential problem for the candidate who is ultimately elected President. Having won office without the active involvement of local, state, and congressional leaders, the new President may lack their support for his policies. Moreover, the skills required to organize, fund and win primary campaigns are not necessarily the kinds of skills required to deal with Congress, the bureaucracy, or foreign governments. It should be noted that the time factor now involved in campaigning for nomination, coupled with the fact that even an incumbent President may easily be challenged, results in the possiblity that a President seeking renomination and reelection may be distracted from his responsibilities to the detriment of the national interest.

There was a forum consensus that steps should be taken to restructure the present system. One area of general agreement was that the selection process—and particularly the primary season—should be made both shorter and more compact. The specific proposals varied, but the thrust was toward a half-year of activity including a series of regional or at least multi-state primaries over perhaps a two month period. No speaker advocated a national primary, since such a development was viewed as one that would probably administer the coup de grace to the party system.

The panelists also agreed that the strengthening of the parties was a necessity and a priority. Most focused in on the need for more professional input in the selection process, and most noted that since democratization had come about through the reform of party rules, the same route might be followed in achieving revision. While there were various proposals for change, the pattern was to increase the proportion of party professionals—both elected officials and party leaders—serving as delegates to national conventions. No one advocated a return to the "boss" system, but there was agreement that the present breakdown of party function and authority must be arrested to prevent total destruction of the party system by the continuing proliferation of primaries.

There were both political and governmental aspects to this concern about the parties. Politically, the absence at national party conventions of state Governors and party chairpersons, of Senators and Representatives, of prominent party elders was seen as depriving the party of the political insight and experience most likely to produce a candidate who is not only representative of the party's constituencies but also capable of winning election. From the view point of governance, it was widely felt that a strong and effective presidency requires structured and effective parties; that the traditional mediational role played by the major parties in bringing diverse groups together for the common purpose of electing a President was also of crucial importance in helping the President lead Congress and the country toward the achievement of national goals.

It was further agreed that the shift to primaries as the key to candidate selection has magnified the influence of the media and of money in American politics. In effect the media—and particularly television—have taken the place of party leaders as the arbiters of the selection process. With a large field of hopefuls and a large number of primaries, the identification of "front-runners" or "winners" is often a matter of interpretation, and the media editor or commentator may therefore play a creative rather than simply a descriptive role in the selection process. Not only did 1980 witness the emergence of a nonparty, media-campaign candidate in John Anderson, it also saw the merger of the media consultant and the campaign manager in his mentor, David Garth. In fact, media consultants have become key figures on the political scene, as have pollsters and fund raisers. Here again there are direct connections to increasing costs and to an emphasis on skills more related to advertising and public relations than to governing.

Many of the panelists were disturbed by the increasing importance of the media, media consultants, and others connected with the technological aspects of the new politics, but most were hard put to come up with any suggestions for changes which would be meaningful. Rules to prevent winner projections and early election reports from influencing those who vote later, or attempts to limit television coverage of primaries were seen as matters for media self-regulation. Moreover, it was generally felt that several of the suggested changes (stronger parties, regional primaries, etc.) would have desirable affects on problems related to the media.

As for the money problem, general approval of public financing as a principle was tempered by the realization that the present system needs revision. Such changes, most speakers thought, should be designed to increase individual contributions in number and amount while limiting the growth and influence of political action committees. The latter change was also directed to curtailing the proliferation and power of single-interest groups. Despite the introduction of public financing for both primary and general election campaigns, the present system has exacerbated the money problem. The reason lies in the limitations imposed on individual contributions to candidates coupled with the freeing of organizational contributions through political action committees (PACs). Because PACs are often directly associated with single-interest groups, financing provisions which encourage their use result in completing a cycle of heavily funded, media-centered, multi-candidate, low-turnout primary elections producing more narrowly based and more ideologically oriented candidates for the general election.

There was great concern among all the panelists with regard to the continuing decline in voter turnout. Party reform has indeed increased the number of citizens who vote in primary elections (30 million in 1980), but it has not similarly affected turnout in general elections. On the contrary, and ironically, the number of people who vote for President has decreased in each election over the past 20 years: 63.5 percent of eligible voters cast ballots in 1960; 61.7 percent in 1968; 55.4 percent in 1972; 54.4 in 1976; and 53.8 percent in 1980. Whatever the causes of this phenomenon may be, the consensus was that more effective parties, better candidates, and a greater sense of both cohesion and purpose in the political system were necessary to stem the tide of indifference.

The question raised in the project's final session ("Is This Any Way to Elect A President?") was, in fact, the question being addressed throughout the two weeks of meetings and seminars. The answer of all who participated in the project was that although the present selection/election process is the product of well-intentioned reforms, it nonetheless needs reforming; that inherent in the current system are defects which could lead to political chaos and governmental impotence; that unless action is taken quickly (certainly well before the next presidential election season begins) the future of American democracy may be endangered.

We hope that this volume will help generate serious discussion about the presidential selection/election process, and that it will be of value in the continuing effort to improve the American political system. Also, we would like the readers to be aware that this volume consists of excerpted transcripts of the original dialogs of the seminars.

I

Understanding Presidential Politics

Jeane J. Kirkpatrick
Austin Ranney
Howard R. Penniman
Norman J. Ornstein
Thomas E. Mann

KIRKPATRICK: When analyzing the presidential selection process, the most important factor to bear in mind is the political effect of the separation of powers in the United States. Our separation of powers is of course complex. Powers are separated vertically between the states and the nation, and horizontally between the legislative, judicial and executive branches of the national government. At the formal level, that is very well known and widely understood.

But the political implications of the reality of separation of powers in this country are frequently missed. The most important of those political consequences is that although the presidential contest takes place in a national arena, primarily through the media, all decisions are made at the state level. The states are the decision-making arena both for nomination politics and for the general election. Their decisions are registered through the electoral college. Never take your eye off what is going on in the states.

The horizontal separation of powers also has important political consequences because presidents can do little without the support of a majority of Congress.

In France, for example, presidents can do something without the National Assembly. There are limits to what they can do, but these limits are not at all like the limits on an American president vis-à-vis the Congress. An American president is heavily dependent upon a shifting, amorphous and very complicated kind of coalition that forms in the Congress. So in thinking about platforms and parties in this country and always is very important to bear in mind the politics that the separation of powers between the legislative and executive branches.

This makes it difficult to adopt policies, and it is supposed to be that way. It is supposed to be difficult for the American federal government to operate. When the president has trouble securing the ratification of a major treaty, that is the way it is supposed to be, there is supposed to be broad consensus before action is possible.

The second general point I would like to make concerns the different relationship between organization and ideology in a country like France and the United States.

In France ideological tendencies are more stable than party organizations (except for the Communist party). In the United States as in Britain, the parties and party identification are more salient and stable than ideology. This means that it is very difficult for a new party to come into being and have much of an impact on political life. This remains true even though party identification has been waning.

Despite the stability of American parties either party can win any presidential contest. Presidential elections since World War II demonstrate that either party can win. Harry Truman, a Democrat was succeeded by Dwight Eisenhower, a Republican who held the White House until John Kennedy, a Democrat was elected. He was followed by Lyndon Johnson another Democrat, who gave way to Richard Nixon, a Republican, and then in 1976 Jimmy Carter, a Democrat was elected. Moreover, the elections of 1968 and 1976 were so close that very small changes in marginal, selective states would have in fact reversed the results of the election.

Unlike France, the U.S. has no major party (such as the Communists) which is a permanent minority party. Finally, another broad difference between French and American politics is that the rhetoric of French politics tends to be more left than the performance of French presidents and legislative parties. The reverse is true in the United States. The rhetoric of American politics seems to be more conservative than the performance, legislative or executive, of either of the parties in office.

These then are a few general factors which are important to note by any observer of our presidential election process.

RANNEY: During the past decade in the United States we have undergone what can only be called a revolution in the manner in which we nominate our presidential candidates. In 1968 and for well over a hundred years before that, American presidential candidates were largely selected by coalitions formed among party leaders, most of whom, were leaders of state political parties and sometimes of large city political parties. The decisions were made by negotiations among a very small group of leaders. That is no longer the case.

The conventions now do not make any decisions. They simply register decisions already made long before they meet, not only with regard to the most important matter—picking the presidential candidates—but with regard to the other major piece of business—the writing and the adoption of the platform—almost all of which takes place long before the convention meets.

Now there have been, I think, two or three proximate causes of this revolution in the presidential nominating process. One of them has been a number of rules changes that the political parties, mainly the Democratic party, but also the Republican, have made. For example, the introduction of proportional representation into our nominating process.

Unlike most European countries, the United States has used proportional representation very little. It has been tried for a few city councils here and there, but it has never had any large scale application except in the choice of delegates to the national nominating conventions. That came from a rule originally adopted by the Democratic party for its 1976 convention, providing that each presidential candidate shall get from a state a number of delegates pledged to him that is proportionate to his share of the vote in the presidential preference primary or in the state convention. There have been a number of other similar rules that the parties have adopted that have had a very powerful impact.

The other proximate cause for the revolution in the nature of the presidential nominating process has been the enormous increase in the number of states holding presidential primaries since 1968. In that year, in which we had the last of the pre-reform conventions, sixteen states and the District of Columbia held presidential primaries, and those presidential primaries together selected about one third of all of the delegates to the national conventions.

That meant that the presidential primaries were only one important element in the process. Sometimes they were quite important, as in the case of John F. Kennedy, who used them to show that a Catholic could be elected in a predominantly Protestant country.

But there were many other occasions in which presidential candidates were nominated without ever even entering a primary. Hubert Humphrey was nominated by the Democrats in 1968 without ever entering a primary. Adlai Stevenson was nominated by the Democrats in 1952 without ever entering a primary.

In 1980, presidential primaries have been held in thirty-seven states, and those primaries have chosen about 80 percent of all of the delegates at both parties' national conventions. That means that the person who wins the nomination wins it not by putting together coalitions of leaders at the conventions, but by winning enough of the votes in those primaries.

The primaries are not all held on one day; they are held sequentially. The whole decision-making process begins in January and does not end until June, but what happens early in the primary campaigning is a lot more important than what happens late. The candidate who does the best in the first third of the selection process is almost surely going to win the nomination. He builds up something that reporters have called "momentum." It is a metaphor drawn from the sports pages and shows that United States political reporting is a subset of sports reporting: the primary concern is with who is ahead and who has momentum. The notion of momentum means that the early winner is almost surely going to win the nomination.

One result this year has been that when only half of the votes that were going to be cast in all of the primaries had been cast, and when less than half of all of the delegates that were to be selected were selected, it was already universally conceded that Jimmy Carter and Ronald Reagan had their respective party nominations all locked up. This means that the nominating conventions are very close to being to the presidential nominating process what the electoral college is to the presidential electing process. They are not decision-making bodies. They are bodies that register decisions that have been made long before they meet.

Finally, the parties have almost completely disappeared from the presidential nominating process. That is to say, there is not now in either party in the United States a group of party leaders who can meet together and conclude that *a, b,* and *c* are absolutely impossible as candidates, and that *x* and *y* are the best possibilities; therefore it has got to be one of those two. The fact is that in both parties the contest is literally wide open, and any candidate who has the right organization, the right strategy, has built up enough credit in the country and has been running for the office long enough (that is very important too) is going to win the nomination regardless of whether the leaders of his party approve of him or for that matter have ever even heard of him.

On the other hand, the nomination that Ronald Reagan won is something that had been campaigning for more or less for twelve years. He has been campaigning for it full time ever since he left the governorship of California in 1974. Jimmy Carter spent two years of full-time, all-out campaigning for the presidential nomination in 1980, and my guess is that any non-incumbent president who would like to be his party's nominee in 1984 had better start getting his campaign organization together, raising money and planning strategy not too long after the November election.

So our system today is very different from the system that existed prior to 1968. Whether it is a better system or a worse system I think depends upon one's basic standards of appraisal. I've come to the conclusion that in the United States there are two basic philosophies from which people approach this question of whether or not the reformed system is better or not than the old unreformed system.

Each position can be characterized by a little epigram. One is characterized by the epigram "virtue is its own reward." People feel that the current system is much more fair, much more democratic, and just much more decent in every way, and they like it. The other is a philosophy whose epigram might be "by their fruits ye shall know them." Those people say that the present system is something approaching a disaster in terms of its destruction of the political parties as anything other than labels, and also in terms of the quality of the candidates.

PENNIMAN: The aspects of presidential politics on which I want to focus are the phenomena of third parties, independent candidates, and—in 1980—John Anderson.

Third parties in the United States in the twentieth century are presidential parties. This was not true of the nineteenth century, when third parties like the Republican party in 1854 and the Populists in 1892 sought legislative and executive offices at all levels—local, state, and national. This remained true for all third parties through 1912 when the Socialist party picked up six percent of the presidential vote, elected members to the House of Representatives and controlled about three or four dozen city governments. But since then large third parties have been presidential parties.

When Anderson runs, he runs without anyone else except his vice-presidential candidate. There will be no Anderson party. He calls himself an independent, but if he had called himself, as George Wallace did, the American Independent party candidate, he would also have supported no candidates for the state and local offices. The reason for all this is basically that candidates for offices below the presidency are selected in party primaries.

These primaries are like the presidential primaries, but their impact on the party at the state and congressional levels has been more important. Primary selection makes the candidates for Congress almost wholly independent of their parties. It means that the United States can have a two-party system because both parties are so fragmented that Congressmen may vote as they wish on legislation rather than accepting party discipline. They can be any kind of people from right to left within the Democratic party or within the Republican party. Because this is true, there is no need to establish a third party to seek office.

As a result, there has been no third party member of the House of Representatives since Vito Marcantonio was elected from New York in 1948. We have gone thirty years without a single third party member in the House of Representatives. Though we had a Conservative party member elected to the Senate in 1970, he was endorsed by the Republican President and tacitly supported by the Republican Governor of New York. In Washington he immediately became part of the Republican conference and in 1976 ran as a Republican with Conservative party support.

John Anderson is going to be like the presidential candidates who have campaigned during the last sixty years of American history. He will be a lone candidate interested in no office but the presidency. In essence, third parties are not parties but protest candidates. A primary can provide a man who satisfies voters in each single-member district, but the Republican and the Democratic presidential candidates may not satisfy the different views of all American voters— especially if the country is divided over some deeply felt issue or issues.

When such a situation occurs, third and fourth candidates may arise to appeal to those not satisfied by the Republican and Democratic candidates. Anderson must turn to these dissatisfied people, if they exist, in search of support. Historically the candidates who have received support enough to get electoral college votes since 1920 have been persons identified with strongly felt regional, oral least state, dissent from national opinions. They have won electoral votes because their support was sufficiently clustered to provide a plurality of the votes in one or more states. Without carrying a plurality of the votes in a state, a candidate gets no electoral votes and one who gets no electoral votes might as well have stayed home except for whatever "educational" value his campaign may have had.

To illustrate what happens, let us look at the 1948 elections when two third-party candidates drew almost exactly the same number of popular votes. Henry Wallace was a national candidate who drew 2.4 percent of the popular votes scattered across the country. Strom Thurmond was a regional candidate who, because of the oddities of American federalism, was on the ballot as a Democratic candidate in four states, not as an independent or a third party candidate. Thurmond carried the four states with his 2.4 percent so he received thirty-nine electoral votes while Wallace's scattered vote of 2.4 percent won no electoral votes.

In 1924, Robert M. LaFollette ran as a third party candidate and got 16.6 percent of the popular vote but carried only his home state of Wisconsin with its thirteen electoral votes. In 1968, George Wallace carried 13.5 percent of the popular vote and got forty-six electoral votes because his vote was heavily concentrated in five states of the Deep South. He had support outside these states, but it was scattered and added nothing to his electoral votes. So Anderson must find states where he can carry a plurality of the popular votes. He is likely to carry the plurality in a state only if voters there are firmly convinced that the two major parties are so close together on important issues that they will cast a protest vote rather than help either major party candidate win. They will waste their vote because the issue is that important to them.

In 1948 and 1968 we had excellent examples of this phenomenon. In both years many voters in the South felt that on civil rights and racial equality (which they opposed) there was "not a dime's worth of difference" between the two major party candidates. So Thurmond carried four states and Wallace five. Now Anderson must find issues so important that people are prepared to say, we will vote for him because we firmly believe that neither of the two major party candidates is attacking the issues in a way acceptable to us and we will protest before voting for either of them. And they have to be voters clustered in a few states, not spread across the country. Otherwise, he may pick up as many as 3 percent, 5 percent, or 10 percent of the popular vote and get no electoral votes.

It is, of course, most unlikely that any independent will win 10 percent of the votes in 1980. He is more likely to win only a handful of popular votes and no electoral votes. It would seem to me also that in late November we will be saying that Anderson was a media event in the spring and summer, here and in Europe and Israel, but not an electoral event in the fall. Henry Wallace had the support of very nearly 25 percent of the votes in the polls in May and June of 1948. He got 2.4 percent of the popular vote in November. In 1968 George Wallace had 25 percent of the popular vote in August and September polls, but six weeks later he won 13.5 percent in the general election. Unless some catastrophe virtually destroys one or both of the major party candidates between now and the election, John Anderson is likely to be only a footnote in the histories of this period.

ORNSTEIN: I think John Anderson has a very reasonable chance of picking up a sizable number of electoral votes in the 1980 election. There is a chance that he may force this election into a situation where the outcome will not be decided on the night of

November 4, 1980, but rather sometime later—either in December when the electors themselves actually meet and unofficially vote to determine whether anybody can get a majority, or in January when the votes of the electors are officially counted in the House of Representatives. If nobody then has a majority, the House immediately begins to ballot by state to determine the next president.

I think the Anderson phenomenon is a little bit different than other third party phenomena. It is different than 1968. It is different than 1948, when we had third party candidates who were essentially on the fringes of American politics; who represented an ideological splinter and who essentially got votes from an ideological splinter. That is not John Anderson. He does not stand on the extreme of the political spectrum, and he is not really appealing to people who feel alienated.

Rather, he appeals to people who think that neither of the major party candidates would make a good president. John Anderson is there and that's what he wants and that's why he is saying "Think about the Anderson difference." He is a different candidate. I do not think issues are going to be terribly important to him. I think he has been handed some issues like the equal rights amendment and similar things that he will use to his benefit, but I do not think that is going to be the basis for his campaign.

My guess is that three things will determine whether Anderson has a chance of picking up a sizable number of electoral votes—and I do not think he needs very many to create a strong chance of throwing this election into the House of Representatives. The first thing is whether or not the League of Women Voters, which runs the televised debates in presidential elections now, decides to allow John Anderson to debate with Jimmy Carter and Ronald Reagan.

Debates create the opportunity for a third party or independent candidate to be seen as an equal and if John Anderson is up there with Jimmy Carter and Ronald Reagan, I think he gets instant credibility.

The second hurdle is choosing a vice-presidential nominee who also has credibility. If John Anderson can choose somebody who is seen by the national media as a strong individual, somebody who has the experience and the talent to be able to step into the presidency himself or herself, then that will give him some credibility and that is what John Anderson needs right now—credibility.

Third, he has to raise money. He has to raise enough money to run a reasonable campaign. The two major party candidates, under the public financing laws, will get about $29.5 million apiece from the federal government to run their campaigns. I do not think John Anderson needs that amount of money to run a reasonable, credible campaign that concentrates on the states and regions where he can pick up electoral votes. My guess is that $10 million would be a good baseline figure.

If he can keep the momentum going in that way, if those three things take place, then I think he has a very strong chance.

I do not think he needs very many electoral votes. The 1976 election, in terms of electoral votes, was quite close between Gerald Ford and Jimmy Carter. My guess would be that the 1980 election, absent Anderson, would turn out fairly much the same way—a close, tight election.

Furthermore, my guess would be that if John Anderson could pick up two or three or four states, he has a very strong chance of preventing anybody from getting a majority. Now what states would those be? I do not think they would be very concentrated regionally. I think we can look at states where there are a sizable number of liberal, activist Democrats combined with moderate to liberal Republicans, and we can look at states which have in the past had some history for independence at one level or another.

New York, for example, has, for some time now, had four parties on the ballot—Democrat, Republican, Liberal, Conservative—and is familiar and comfortable with alternatives other than the two major parties. John Anderson has a chance of capturing a plurality of votes in such a state.

I think Anderson also has a strong chance of taking Massachusetts. I think he has a strong chance of taking Connecticut, of taking Wisconsin, very possibly of taking Minnesota or Oregon.

What would happen if John Anderson did manage to throw the election into the House of Representatives? This has not happened in a long, long time. The last time was in the 1824 election, and it was fascinating because the eventual winner in the House of

Representatives, John Quincy Adams, was not the leader at the time of the election in popular votes or in electoral votes. He finished second in both and yet managed to move up and be selected as president. The original leader in those two categories, and the disgruntled loser, was Andrew Jackson, who said afterwards that there had never been such corruption and wheeling and dealing anywhere in the history of the world. He retreated and planned his comeback and evidently enough of the American people agreed because he was elected by a landslide four years later.

In any event, the constitutional election process can be very complex. The general election in November does not choose individuals or presidents; it chooses electors. It chooses them on a state by state basis and to be elected it is necessary to get a majority of the electoral votes. The electors, who tend to be leaders of one sort or another in their communities, meet a month or so later in the middle of December and actually cast votes for president.

Some state laws bind their votes but we have had many instances in the past where electors have voted for somebody entirely different from the candidate they represented on the ballot. And that is not illegal. So if nobody gets a majority of the electoral votes on election day, the focus is going to turn first to the electors' voting in December.

It is possible that a deal between Anderson and Reagan or Anderson and Carter could be worked out between November and December. But I think that is unlikely. Thus the focus would more likely shift to January 6th, which under law is when the electoral votes are officially counted.

At that point if nobody has a majority, then according to the Constitution the House of Representatives—and it would be a new House also elected in November—would meet, break into state delegations, and each would try to work out its vote as an individual state. There would be fifty votes that could be cast in the House of Representatives. They could choose only from among the top three in electoral votes, so there is a choice of three individuals involved.

Right now, the Democrats control twenty-nine of the fifty state delegations, the Republicans twelve, and nine are evenly divided by party. It is likely that after this election, there will still be a majority of state delegations controlled by the Democrats, but it is also likely for one reason or another that some members will not simply vote the party line. That creates a strong possibility of nobody being selected by the House of Representatives because you need a majority of the states—twenty-six—voting for one individual to elect a president.

If such a deadlock should occur in the House, our attention would turn to the Senate, where from among the top two persons with electoral votes for vice president an election is held simultaneously with the presidential vote in the House. Here there would be less of a problem, since there would probably be a clear Democratic majority, and voting individually the Senators would have chosen Walter Mon-dale, who could become Acting President.

But there is yet another scenario. For, if neither house can make a choice, by law the Speaker of the House of Representatives—Tip O'Neill—becomes Acting President. Or, finally, Congress could pass a law making someone else Acting President.

If we just take the most likely possibility, however, we could see Walter Mondale as Acting President for two years, when the House of Representatives is again elected, changes its composition and votes again. Or if the House deadlock was ended for one reason or another, perhaps if one House member died during the course of the year and that shifted one state, then they could very possibly choose somebody else, since according to the Constitution at any time during the four-year term, they can vote and put in a new President-elect. My guess is frankly that if we reach that situation, with Walter Mondale as Vice President-elect and Acting President, the House would stop meeting and voting on this issue and say all right this is just the way it is going to be for four years and we will try and reach a mandate four years from now.

None of this may happen but it is something to be sensitive to because the Anderson candidacy does raise the possibility of creating an unprecedented situation in twentieth century American politics.

MANN: One of the curious aspects of American politics is that we spend at least two years nominating and electing a president. We put an enormous amount of public attention and media budgets into it and we heighten expectations about the importance of who is President of these United States.

And then we confront a successful candidate with the office of the presidency and a constitutional structure with a clear separation of powers and an extraordinarily important institution called Congress that has much to do with the governance of this country. After all this, the natural course of events is to have the same media that focused all of our attention on this process of nominating and electing a President take on the task of demonstrating how unsuccessful that particular incumbent is in leading our country.

In any event we ought to pay a little bit of attention to the other elections that are going on in 1980 because they are really quite interesting and important. We have thirty-four Senate seats up in 1980. We have 435 House elections. We have a number of gubernatorial races and a large number of state legislative races.

The latter may not seem terribly important, but it is, in two respects. One, because of the importance of who controls the state legislatures in the aftermath of the decennial census. We have a census in 1980, and after the census, we reapportion seats in the House of Representatives, and before we elect the new House in 1982 we redistrict—that is, we redraw the boundaries of virtually every congressional district. The authority for redrawing those lines is vested in state legislatures (with the governor able to veto or approve) and so the political geography of congressional districts will be decided in the fifty states over the next two years. Therefore the outcome of the state legislative races and the gubernatorial races in 1980 will be extraordinarily important for the shape of national politics in the 1980's. So we ought to pay some attention to that.

We always talk about the two party system in American politics, but we do not really have a two party system; we have a one and one-half party system. We have the Democratic party which competes successfully on the presidential and congressional levels, and then we have the Republican party which has been remarkably successful competing for the presidency, but remarkably unsuccessful in seeking to control the House and the Senate of the U.S. Congress. We have seen twenty-five years of unbroken Democratic control of both the House and the Senate.

In fact we can go all the way back to 1932 and find that in the intervening period, we have only had a couple of Congresses in which the Republicans have controlled one or both houses. It has been a remarkably unsuccessful record for the Republican party and why that has happened is one of the curiosities of our politics. It is especially curious to Republican members of Congress, who have become so accustomed to their minority status that they act in ways within the institution that reflect their being without responsibility and out of power for so long.

Now one of the interesting things about the 1980 elections, it seems to me, is the extent to which people are paying attention to the control of the Congress and not just the presidency. Some people care more than others, but there has been a lot of talk by Republicans in particular about the importance of an entire Republican ticket succeeding, and especially of a Republican Congress.

We have gone through elections in our recent history in which the top of the ticket made virtually no mention of the rest of the ticket.

Perhaps the clearest example of this is the 1972 election, when Richard Nixon was running for reelection against George McGovern. In that election Richard Nixon was swept into office in a landslide, but the Republicans won only 46 percent of the national vote for the House and picked up only 12 seats.

That points to a fundamental change in congressional elections—namely, elections for Congress have become increasingly separated from elections for the presidency. Moreover, congressional elections have become more localized, more insulated from national events such as the state of the economy. The main reason is that we have elected a new cadre of individuals to the Congress, who have become extremely adept at running as individuals; not necessarily as Democrats or Republicans, but as individual entrepreneurs with their own cottage industry campaign organizations, utilizing all of the varied resources of incumbency.

Current members of the United States Congress, especially those in the House of Representatives, have developed ways to get close to the people, communicate with them, convey to them their sincere conviction about all sorts of things. It began by candidates some years ago walking hundreds of miles across their congressional districts and states, shaking hands with people and showing that they were regular folk. Then came the "work day," that is an occasion when a candidate for Congress puts on a hard hat and goes out to the construction site and drives a crane for a day, sees what the regular people think and believe and what their concerns are.

Of course it is reasonable for those who run for office to get close to the people, but now as long as they are out there, they figure why do it in isolation, why not notify the three local television and radio stations and the weekly and daily newspapers. So suddenly it is a major media event. In addition to work days, we have town meetings and mobile offices. The Canadians have adopted the northern version of the mobile offices—a canoe trip through the Northwest Territories. In any case, members of Congress have increasingly adopted what one scholar, Richard Fenno, calls "home styles," in which they develop a personal relationship with the people in their district so that the electoral choice has nothing to do with presidential politics, parties or national issues, but very much comes down to a question of trust: Do you trust this individual to do what is right, to care, to listen, to be concerned and so on.

As a consequence, we have lost national accountability, a situation in which elections authorize a party to govern and then stand on the record of their governance. Instead, we have completely separated the objective output of the legislature from the conditions for being reelected. They are really quite separated and that explains in large part the difficulty presidents have in moving legislative programs through Congress. It is not that members of Congress are insensitive to public opinion. To the contrary, they are hypersensitive to public opinion in representing their local constituents' concerns.

There is a widespread belief that because of the impressive advantages of incumbency and because of the fact that we have more people who identify as Democrats than as Republicans, it is impossible for the Republicans ever to overcome their minority status in Congress. That is the conventional wisdom in political science and politics generally. On the other hand, there is feeling among some that this year may be different and that the 1980's may lead to a reversal of some of these trends in congressional elections.

Let me mention several of the factors involved. The Republicans have a very intelligent, well developed strategy for reaching a majority status in the Congress that they have been working on since 1976, under the leadership of Bill Brock, Chairman of the Republican National Committee.

The Republican National Committee is a very large, vibrant, active organization that raises lots of money and provides marvelous services, not just to presidential candidates, but down the line. These things are part of the Republican strategy for gaining control of Congress. They have a national media campaign on which they have spent $5 million this year running ads which make fun of Speaker Tip O'Neill and which try to educate the public that the Democrats have controlled Congress for twenty-five years.

People do not really know that. They tend to view the control of American politics through the presidency and they often do not focus on which party is in control of the Congress. The Republicans are trying to undo that. They are trying to educate the American people that the Congress is important for policymaking, that it has been controlled by Democrats for many years and that it is time for change. It is a very sophisticated strategy.

Another part of the Republican strategy is that for the first time in many years, we have a linking of presidential and congressional campaigns. We saw it when candidate Reagan's tax cut proposal was orchestrated with Republicans in Congress, and we will see it time and time again. Reagan will try to convince the American people that they need also to elect Republicans to Congress so that his program has an opportunity to be passed and tested.

Still a further aspect of Republican strategy is that they have been very active in recruiting good candidates for the House and the Senate. It is something that they failed to do in the past. Throughout the 1970's it was difficult for the Republicans to find good candidates for Congress. Part of it was the political mood, the atmosphere.

While Harvard is not typical of American society or American universities, in 1972, the presidential preference poll on campus showed something like George McGovern 90 percent, Richard Nixon 10 percent. By 1976, it was more like Jimmy Carter 55 percent, Gerald Ford 45 percent. It was very, very close. It became respectable to be a Republican on campus again.

These former students are moving into state legislative races, into local community politics. Some of the best talent is coming into the Republican party now. The national Republicans are seeking them out, helping them raise money, training them in modern campaign technologies, and that is beginning to make a difference and will continue to make a difference throughout the early part of the 1980's.

The Republicans are active in financing challenges, and this is important because the reason that 95 percent of House incumbents win reelection every two years is primarily because they are not challenged; there may be a nominal candidate, but there is no serious race made against them. The average expenditure of challengers in 75 percent of the races with incumbents running is less than $40,000. In American politics, that is nothing. I mean no one learns your last name for $40,000. A serious race costs well over $100,000 and in many congressional districts $200,000, $300,000, $400,000. Republicans finally are beginning to realize that if good challengers are well financed, many of the advances of incumbency will fall by the wayside. So they are making progress.

Finally, the Republicans have been making an effort to elect more members in the state legislative races in order to have an influence on the drawing of congressional district boundaries in preparation for the 1982 election.

All of these factors taken together—combined with the fact that the issues and concerns of the American people right now smell like Republican issues and concerns—could bring about a basic change in the pattern of our politics. Indeed, I would suggest that these factors make it likely that the Republicans will make substantial gains in the 1980 elections. They stand to gain in the House and in the Senate also, because there are many more Democratic senators up for reelection (24) than Republicans (only 10). I would look for a gain of anywhere from three to six seats in the Senate, giving the Republicans a majority if not in partisan terms, then in ideological terms. In the House, I look for a pick-up of twenty to twenty-five seats for the Republicans. Right now in the House there are 275

Democrats and 159 Republicans. Twenty or twenty-five seats will still leave the Republicans over forty short of control, but then they will look to the 1982 and 1984 elections for consolidating and increasing their 1980 gains. Over the long run, if things break right for them, the Republicans have the first realistic chance they have had since 1952 of once again becoming the majority party in both Houses of the United States Congress.

II

The Electoral System: Voters, Parties, Candidates

Richard M. Scammon
Carol Bellamy

SCAMMON: A brief word about the nature of the American electorate, and I am speaking now only of people who vote. The abstentions do not count in American politics any more than they do in politics anywhere else. The only good voter is a live voter; the others you can ignore.

The turnout of voters in America is not very high. About 55 percent of the total adult population. But the 55 percent takes as its base every person living in this country over eighteen, thus including aliens, both legal and illegal; it includes people who have not fulfilled the citizenship residency requirement and so on. So that we normally estimate about two-thirds of our people vote; one-third do not.

Now who are the people who vote? They are in the main metropolitan. But not from the center city. Basically, the voter is a person who lives in suburbs, in the settled areas of the large cities, or in the small cities.

I suppose the two major social changes in America since the war would be, first, the flight from the land and the diminishment of the agricultural population, and second, the flight from the core city and the diminishment of its political and economic influence.

The city is still important, but it is nowhere nearly as important as it was, say, in the days of Roosevelt. The basis of American political power is now found in the outlying areas, the residential areas of the cities, in the suburbs and in the smaller cities of the country. It is 90 percent white, about 9 percent black, about 1 percent Japanese-American, Chinese-American, American Indian, Filipino, and so on.

The average age of the voters is around 47. This is not the politics of youth, this is the politics of the middle-aged. If you want to win office, you would be glad to have 100 percent of every age group. But if you have to make a choice, you go for the people over 50, not for those under 30. If you got all the people over 50 to vote for you, while all the people under 30 voted against you, you would win so easily that the next time you could not raise any campaign money because everybody would figure you did not need any help.

It is an electorate in which the majority of voters are women. But not by a great deal; about 51-49. The overage of women in the total population is much greater than that, probably four or five percent more. But voting turnout is somewhat less among women percentage-wise than it is among men, and the net result is that the electorate in a presidential year is about 51-49, women.

This occasionally makes a difference, but by and large, gender as an issue is not that important. The issues tend to be more related to history, personality, party and to strike across the sex line. It is rather difficult to find any election in America which is determined with all the men on one side and all the women on the other. In fact I do not know of any. Sometimes you get a bit more overage of men as opposed to women, but basically just gender as gender is not that important.

This electorate is also in many ways centrist in nature. I do not speak now of New York City any more than I would speak of a conservative area like northern Louisiana. But nationally, the electorate tends to be middle-aged, middle class, and middle minded. The high school diploma is still the norm, although educational level is rapidly increasing, and more and more you are getting people who have at least a couple of years of college, which does not mean they are any smarter, it just means that they have been there for two more years. In fact the United States Census Bureau has a wonderful phrase in its asking of questions. It does not ask: "How much education have you received?" It asks: "How many years did you attend school?"

In the present political process the typical voter is a woman, middle-aged, white, lower middle class, either working herself or married to a skilled worker, living in the suburbs, and probably having lived there for a good length of time.

We find that one of the best ways to measure voter turnout in America is to inquire whether or not the person in the house we visit has lived there more than six years. Among people who have lived in a place more than six years, with these other characteristics you may get as much as an eighty or ninety percent turnout.

But it is very interesting that young people are very low voters. In fact their turnout is lower than people in their eighties; probably because young people here, as elsewhere in the world, are foot-loose, they have not really settled down yet, maybe they are serving in the army, maybe they are still pursuing a college education. They have not yet settled down to the point at which they have established families. Another good test of non-voting is that if you have a family with children, and if the husband is old enough to have paid the first bill to get his children's teeth fixed, they are probably voters, because this has established a life and social and economic pattern which tends to produce more turnout.

Let me move now to the general circumstances of the election year. A presidential election in America is a peculiar and unique kind of experience, because unlike most other elections in this country, the candidates for the office of the presidency are elected indirectly by an electoral college, which although it is largely a legal fiction is still there. And they are nominated for this political office in the two major political parties by conventions. Almost every other nominating activity in this country takes place through primary elections. Only two or three states nominate congressmen, senators, governors, mayors, presidents of the city council, aldermen, state legislators, by any system except the primary. And the primary has been the prime factor of differentiation between American and European politics for the last seventy-five years. I say differentiation, because with a primary election it is absolutely impossible to maintain any really effective kind of party discipline, party organization, or party control.

The basic authority of party is always the power to nominate—who can put the party label after the name of the candidate? The only person who can do that in America is the voter. And the voter can be appealed to by anybody. The result is that you will get in both the Republican and Democratic parties very, very wide variations of ideological commitment from the far right to the far left. You will get people gathered together under this gaudy umbrella of every conceivable kind of political view.

In particular, you will find differentiations from area to area. A Democrat who runs for the Congress in New York must have a very different view of the world than a Democrat who runs for Congress in Mississippi. If the Mississippi candidate adopted the New York view, he would be defeated, and if the New York candidate adopted the Mississippi view, he would be defeated. Now they are both Democrats. No, strike that; I do not know what a Democrat is. They are both people whose names are on the ballot with the word *Democrat* after it. But when they get to Congress they go their separate ways, and this is why some people refer to our congressional system as "Balkan," one composed of four hundred thirty-five individual representatives in the House and one hundred in the Senate, occasionally recognizing one another but not necessarily related because of common party affiliation.

Now the presidency is really the only national office. The congressmen do represent their constituencies of about half a million each; the senators represent their states, but only the president represents the whole nation. The presidential candidates are nominated by the two party conventions, with an occasional third candidate like, for example, John Anderson this year, or George Wallace in 1968, or LaFollette in 1924.

The two conventions, up until about fifteen or twenty years ago, were largely representative of what I would call the party leadership, that is those who are concerned with party politics on a regular basis, who went to the caucuses and the meetings and the conventions and so on, and selected delegates. But there began to be introduced way back, about the time of the First World War, a different system of selection in which delegates who went to the national conventions were actually elected by the people who went to the polls as Democrats and as Republicans in primary elections. In the last fifteen or twenty years this has produced a very different kind of nominating process, and the reason is that under the old system, perhaps two to three percent of the normal party faithful would go to these caucuses and choose the people who are going to the national conventions to nominate the candidates. Now that group is up to about twenty or thirty percent.

In the primary elections that have just been finished, there were some thirty-two million votes cast in the Republican primaries and Democratic primaries, and this excluded some fairly large non-primary states. For example, it excluded half the New York constituency and it excluded all the Michigan constituency. I would estimate that in the states which had primary elections, of those people who probably will vote in November, half of them participated in the choice of the candidate.

And I say choice of the candidate, because more and more, the people who want to be delegates are elected in these states that have primaries on the basis of who they are going to vote for in the summer at the convention. In fact, in some states, these candidates for delegate do not even have their names on the ballot. You vote for Carter or for Kennedy or for Reagan or for Bush, and then those delegates are assigned later to the candidates.

What has happened in fact is that the nominating procedure has been taken out of the hands of the party leadership at the local, county, state, national level, and been transferred over to the general public. Let me provide a specific example. In 1952, when Adlai Stevenson was the Democratic nominee for the presidency, Senator Estes Kefauver of Tennessee had run in the few primaries that were available to him—ten or a dozen—and he had won all but one. But when he got to the convention in 1952, he was pushed aside by the party leadership who selected Stevenson.

In 1980 that would not be possible. If you had a situation in which any candidate had gone to the electorate in thirty-six primaries and had won thirty-two of those primaries, he would automatically be nominated, because he would have so many committed delegates, it would be impossible for anyone to deny him the selection.

Some people favor this change, some people oppose it, but I am describing it to you as something different.

Traditionally the major task of the convention is to choose a candidate for the presidency. Now there are a great many other activities that go on there. Members of the national committee are elected for future leadership of the party. A platform is adopted. But this party program, declaration of principles, whatever you want to call it, is not very important. It does represent some kind of political balance, but normally what comes out as the party program is a very innocuous statement.

What really counts are the political views of the candidate as he expresses them from the time of his nomination and his acceptance of that nomination right up to election day. In making my own personal choice on the presidency, I will listen to Anderson and I will listen to Reagan if he is the Republican nominee, and I will listen to Mr. Carter, presuming he is the Democratic nominee, and make a judgment.

Quite honestly, although I have been watching politics and specializing in politics for twenty-five years, I will not read either party platform. Not deliberately, but simply because with a limited amount of time I do not have time to go back and read the Oz books or Sherlock Holmes any more either, and they are more entertaining.

In any event, the problem is the nomination. Not the vice presidential nomination, because this is normally recommended by the presidential candidate. And the presidential candidate's recommendation is always accepted. It is regarded as his first act of leadership to select someone to run with him as his partner.

Everything at the convention hinges around that voting for the president. In fact, if it is as easy to determine as it is now with the Republicans, a very real problem presents itself to both the convention management and the television and radio networks—how do you hold attention to a convention where the major issue is already decided? They have speeches and they have parades and they have song sessions and they introduce the old leaders of the party. (If Mr. Landon, who was the Republican candidate in 1936, is able, he might come and give another speech.) But there is a real problem, especially for television when you do not have a contest. Because while the three major networks will cover these conventions all evening long, the non-network stations can run anything they want, so they will put on an old movie—one I always like is Elvis Presley and the Moon Maids—and the convention audience goes way down. Now if you have a contest, as you did in 1976 with the Republicans, and you really get something interesting going on, then people will tune in.

On the Republican side this year the only thing really of conflict and interest is the choice of a vice presidential candidate and that will be announced by Mr. Reagan. His choice, I am sure, will be approved.

On the Democratic side there has been a much more active contest. Mr. Kennedy is still trying for the nomination. He is trying to persuade some of the delegates who were elected to vote for Mr. Carter that they ought to change their mind, that the situation has changed, that Carter will lose, that his own successes in the last series of primaries on June third when he won a majority of the nine contested elections, that these factors have changed the situation and they ought to move over. This is very unlikely. A man or woman who has been elected to go to New York and cast a vote for Carter has been elected almost always and entirely on that basis, not because their judgment is good or because they are smart. I do not elect a delegate to make judgments. I elect a delegate to do what I want him to do. Vote for Kennedy, vote for Carter.

I must say I think if Kennedy were in the lead and Carter number two, Carter would probably also be asking that people must vote on conscience, get away from the binding effect, and so on.

The binding effect is the natural result of some years of effort by the Democratic reform element to take the nomination away from the leadership and put it in the hands of the people. I am not sure the reform element were really sure that this is what would happen, that Carter would beat Kennedy if you took it to the people but that is what is happening, and they are stuck with it. They are still trying, and they may very well make a good fight of this on the rules that govern the convention with respect to commitment. My own guess is that they will lose.

The Kennedy people, representing the liberal wing of the Democratic party, may also make issues of several matters in the platform, particularly I would think on nuclear power and perhaps on the draft, and certainly on the question of social spending. What their fate may be I don't know. It might make the convention more interesting, but then Democratic conventions are usually more hectic, less organized, more confused and therefore more interesting than the Republican which tend to be fairly middle class, respectable, quiet and white. It is a lot more interesting to watch the Democrats in action.

In addition to the major party nominating process, this year, we have self-selection as another possible avenue to the presidency. This is John Anderson who is a member of Congress from a rural area of northern Illinois. For many years he sat in the Congress as a very conservative member, identified as anti-labor, pro-Vietnam war, pro-nuclear, almost everything that you think he would not be as of now. I think it is best typified by the president of the AFL-CIO, who was asked if the labor movement would endorse Anderson, and he thought for a moment and said, "Holy God, no." That might change.

Anderson today has a rather special constituency as far as we can identify it from polling. People who intend to vote for Anderson now are largely the kind of people who if they were Democrats would have preferred Kennedy over Carter. It is an upper middle-class constituency, fairly wealthy, young, white, living in the suburbs, at least one and usually two college degrees, members of the professional-managerial class, not workers, not farmers, not the elderly, not Black, and a large share of Jewish voters with humanistic tendencies.

Now the difficulty with Anderson of course is what would be true of any candidate who appears very quickly on the scene. Anderson's politics are in the eyes of the beholder. You look at this lump of clay on the sculptor's stand and you sort of move it and, ah he is a liberal; move it a little more and, he is conservative. Now that will change as Anderson gets a better hearing and very likely gets into the debates. At least when he gets onto the TV, gets interviewed and so on, we will probably get a good deal more clarification on what he does believe and think.

His basic appeal is that he is not Reagan and not Carter, and under those conditions he gets a good deal of support. How it will be in October—which normally in America is called the "return-of-the-natives" month, in which people who have been toying with the idea of voting for somebody else move back to a more traditional loyalty—is hard to predict. I just have no idea, because much of the result of this election in November between Reagan and Carter will depend on how many votes Anderson gets and from whom he draws these votes; if he does go down in numbers of supporters, as most people expect, for whom will the remnant who were for Anderson vote? Or if he goes up, could he supplant Carter as the second candidate behind Reagan? He wouldn't supplant Reagan, because Reagan has a solid core of conservative support. But Carter as a centrist has a mixed and less reliable base, and if Reagan, Carter and Anderson are all in it, Anderson could become number two. And that could change everything, because there is a very real tendency in American politics, when you have three candidates, for people supporting the third candidate to say, well here it is October 20th and I do not want to throw my vote away. I am not really an ideological voter, I do not want to commit suicide like Wagner's Seigfried at the end of the fourth act at midnight, you know, and do a great heroic thing. So they choose number one or number two.

If anyone were to ask me who will win, I would say I have not the slightest idea. We have got nearly four months to go until the election. The selection process has fairly well run out, although there are always possibilities for an upset. I do not know what is going to happen in the next four months. Reagan is not a young man, he might become ill. Any of them might become ill. Things may change. New issues might appear; new international crises might affect the election. The economy, a major issue this year, might get better, but quite possibly might also get worse. So all you can do is say that if you are betting, do not. There are no data on which you can base a rational evaluation at this time.

BELLAMY: To begin with a couple of comments on the nature of the American electorate. What else would one have expected, but an average person? I do not subscribe to the theory of an elected public official, Senator Hruska, regarding an unsuccessful candidate for the United States Supreme Court, a fellow by the name of Haynesworth, a number of years ago that we need mediocre judges for mediocre people. And so it is not my view that you need mediocre public officials for mediocre people, if that is the implication of the term *average voter.*

Now I do not mean that in terms of political philosophy; I assume enormous diversity in political philosophy, but it seems to me a degree of intellect is not an uncommon desire, or should not be an uncommon desire.

Mr. Scammon has talked about the impact of the changes in the convention system, and these changes have come very much from the so-called reform element of the Democratic party. I should tell you that here in New York the reform group is known by the initials NDC, or New Democratic Coalition, known by those who have been in politics longer, as November Doesn't Count. I come out of that so-called reform movement, but that quip gives you some idea of how effective we have been.

The one area in which we have clearly been effective is in the rules reform. But it is my view that it is not so much these rules changes, but rather the impact of what I call the new technology that has very much caused the effective disappearance of the party system in this country. By the new technology I mean the media, and particularly TV; radio to some degree, but particularly television. The pencil-press is still around, but post-Watergate everybody needs to be an investigative reporter, so there is no discussion of issues, even assuming issues were important, and I do not think issues play a role in the determination of candidates at all.

As for polling, with all due respect, I find polling to be an appalling technique today because I think people lie. I do not think people tell the truth. I think what they are telling the people who do the polling is what they heard on the six o'clock news the night before, and it may be in fact at that very moment their view.

I think the techniques of polling are very well developed techniques and careful techniques. In fact we are really very sophisticated in the way of polling, but I am troubled about the results of polling given the impact of the media.

But back to television. I have been very successful with television so I probably should not complain, but I will complain in any case because I think television can deal with nothing that vaguely resembles anything very complex that may have a major impact. What happens basically in this country is that we have an hour of news each night, and from a political perspective it is as though—this is my analogy—one has to analyze a tree every day. If I look at a tree one day and I look at a tree six months from now, it may be different, and I can say that six more branches came or something fell off or the tree got five feet taller. But if I look at that tree every day, I do not see much difference. But if I have an hour to fill—not a whole hour, the first twenty minutes I can talk about stabbings and muggings-everyday, for a portion of that time in that television program I have to analyze that tree.

I am not sure problems are more complex today than they have ever been, but the rapid nature of the analysis of everything is, I think, very lacking in substance. We have terribly ill-informed members of the media, as we have terribly ill-informed elected public officials. Maybe the burden is greater on us, but in fact the perceived legitimacy of the media person is much greater, and so what that individual says or conveys in twenty seconds takes on enormous importance.

Direct mail is another part of the new technology. And that gets us to the money involved, the cost and the impact on costs of the new technology which is just enormous.

The costs of campaigns today are incredible. Certainly the presidential candidates' use of the new technologies—television in particular—means the costs are just enormous. So how does the candidate raise the money?

The candidates raise the money by involving themselves with one other thing that I wanted to talk about, the PACs (political action committees). These are basically organizations set up by any number of groups including corporations and labor unions, to raise funds. I am not against anybody giving money, I should tell you, but I think we ought to get back to some kind of restrictions. My view is that there should be no campaign financing unless it is absolute. Once you have the slightest hole in public campaign financing, you do not have real public financing, and you fool yourself if you leave loopholes.

Those are the things that I think affect politics today very much: the new technologies, and the costs of these new technologies, and the impact of having to raise money to meet these kinds of costs.

To add just a few other comments—as for the "typical voter" who turns out to be a woman. In fact we are talking about 44 million women in this country who are now holding down some kind of a job, mostly becuse they need to, and the increasing number of single-parent families, which usually means a woman too. I do not know what the political impact of this will be.

I do not say this is revolutionary, but possibly it might cause some kind of interesting phenomena in the political process. I do not know. I do not mean that women will immediately march out and vote for women candidates; that has not happened in this country. I think perception of female candidates has changed slightly so there is not overt opposition to them now. I think attitudes are getting a little bit more favorable, in part because everybody is angry at politicians. As the woman is not seen as the traditional politician, she picks up votes accordingly. Women have no monopoly on goodness or justice certainly, any more than anyone else, but the number of women in the labor force today may have some impact in future elections.

As to the parties—I think parties are really almost irrelevant. Pressure groups, and the impact of pressure-group money, are the major components of politics today.

I know in this country everybody deplores single interest groups, but they exist and they are very important. I will give you my proposition for dealing with single interest groups. Maybe this is terrible because I hold a position now where I have a constituency of seven million people and with a large constituency you are more isolated from single-interest group pressure. So it is easier for me to say, but it is my view that the way you deal with single-interest politics today is that the person elected to office does not deplore the fact that single-interest politics exists, but has got to bear up and make decisions. I think that we have become paralyzed in decision-making in this country. But how you deal with single-interest politics is not to try and cause it to disappear, although I do not like it, but the individual in politics has to deal with single-interest politics.

One final comment: in American elections this year there is a place that people are not looking at but ought to be interested in, namely the state legislative bodies. These are the legislative bodies that will draw the new district lines that will prevail for state legislatures and Congress for at least the next five years. And to the extent that we have become parochial—so that city fights suburb and suburb fights ex-urb, and sunbelt fights snow belt—who is in Congress and what Congress does is very much determined by what the lines are.

III

The Electoral System: Media and Money

Edward N. Costikyan
John W. McGarry

COSTIKYAN: I would like to focus on why the media have become so important in American politics. Basically the media have been filling a tremendous vacuum. Starting in about 1960-65 the American political party system began to decline for quite complicated reasons, having to do with economic and geographical mobility. It had to do with the availability of other pathways to financial success and social success. It had to do with changing attitudes about parties and politics. But the end result is that today in the United States if you look at the political process and try to identify a party leader you will not find one. The party leaders or party bosses of twenty years ago do not exist. The last one was Mayor Daley of Chicago who died three years ago and his organization could not even carry that city for its candidates this year.

There is no party structure left that amounts to anything. Once there was a hierarchy of party leadership and the party leaders had a great deal to say about who got nominated and a great deal to say about who got elected, because through that party structure the party could reach voters and could persuade them to vote for this candidate or that candidate. But that is all gone.

Finally there is very little party loyalty left. People do not really vote as Democrats or Republicans. They may identify themselves as such, but the percentage of the American public that identify themselves as either Republicans or Democrats has dropped very drastically and even that identification means very little when they get to the voting booth.

Now as a product of all this, politicians have come to realize that if they want to have political and governmental careers, party activity is not particularly significant. And one of the little rules that emerged from the writing of my book on the politics of the 1980's was the fact that if you want to launch a political career through party activity it is like trying to learn to swim with a lead wet suit. You are going to sink.

What has replaced the party is the electronic media. Basically television on a national level; radio more on a local level because the costs are lower and the costs of television are too high to justify its use.

The principal tools that a candidate has to reach the voters are television and radio—not party workers, not the party, not the press, but those two tools. They do a very good job at bringing into somebody's living room the picture and the image of the candidate that the candidate wants to project if he has the money to project it. But they do a dreadful job at persuading people to vote. And a by-product of the decline of the machine which once did perform the function of getting everybody on the block to vote on election day is that the percentage of people who vote in this country has been dropping year after year. A typical result of this phenomenon is the 2.7 percent of the Democratic voters of Iowa that President Carter won in 1976 in what was recognized as a national victory, and launched his rise to the presidency by really putting him on the map nationally.

In looking at numbers we find a lot of deceptive aspects though. First of all our population figures are ten years out of date and there is a lot of extrapolation that has to go on to try and figure out what the population really is. Secondly, the press and the media never report the percentage of the people who vote; they are not interested in that. It is more important that so-and-so got 44 percent of the vote than it is that only 10 percent of the eligibles bothered to vote, even though so-and-so really only got 4.4 percent of the potential vote.

Nevertheless within those constraints you can see a pattern that has emerged starting in 1960, and continuing through '64, '68, '72, '76 and '80: the percentage of people who voted in presidential elections has dropped from something like 68 percent in 1964 to 54 percent in 1976 and the trend is down, and while no one can predict what will happen in 1980 because of the presence of a third possible candidate, I think anyone who has analyzed the figures would say that without Anderson in the picture, or if Anderson turns out not to be a real candidate, the percentage that is likely to vote will drop under 50 percent and perhaps substantially so.

Similar numbers exist if you take the off-year gubernatorial and state elections starting in 1966, and continuing through '70, '74, and '78. By 1978 the nationwide percentage of people who turned out to vote in those elections was 38 percent, having dropped from well over 55 percent.

If you go to municipal elections you get even more startling numbers. In New York City in 1977 the percentage of people who voted was somewhere around 25 percent. Our mayor got 12 percent or about half, and if you look at the percentages that our elected officials have gotten you find strange numbers. Governor Byrne in New Jersey got elected by 15 percent of the eligibles. Governor Carey in New York got elected by 28 percent, and President Carter's percentage in '76 was 27 percent.

Now as all of this happens the intensity of media campaigning increases, because you are trying to reach fewer and fewer people and you use this one available tool and the costs multiply and multiply which has become a major reason why the federal government has intervened in the federal election process. As far as the primary election process and non-federal elections, however, a major task of every candidate is to raise money in order to be able to finance media activity. The current wisdom is that 90 percent of the funds raised should go into television. I question the wisdom of that because television does not reach the vast number of non-voters who could turn any election upside down—but that is the current wisdom.

I will not tell you how to raise money because I do not really know. Everybody invents a new system every four years or every two years. But rock concerts are very good. Finding celebrities who will put on a concert or some kind of performance is very good. Tennis matches are good. Little cocktail parties where people are invited to come and contribute $250 are effective. Direct mail has been used with mixed success. Everybody invents new ways to do it.

In any event this process, centered on raising money, is very different from the political process that once existed. And what is most significant to me is what do you do with that money?

The emphasis on the media as the technique to reach the voters has created a whole new industry in the United States: media expertise with specialists who can create the kind of image that the candidate wants to project into voters' living rooms. Theirs is a new art form, quite different from the methods thirty or forty years ago. The specialists in this technique do more than just take a candidate and say tell me what you want to do and then I will do it for you. The media men increasingly tell the candidate what the candidate wants to do. And the media peoples' ideas are shaped largely by the polls they take. But since the polls traditionally exclude all the non-voters, they have a rather narrowing impact on what kind of images you are going to project. Nonetheless nobody can run a campaign at the national level or the state level and probably not even on the Congressional level without the assistance of one of these people who put together an image and get it into somebody's house.

There are different ways to do it. I focus on television although radio is not that different. Basically there are two approaches.

One is free and one is paid for. The free coverage is what we call news; although it is not news but spectacle. It is really not news that a candidate walked down the street with Gina Lollobrigida or with Pope John Paul or anyone else. I mean it is interesting, but they do not do anything except walk down the street and shake hands. That is not news. That is spectacle, and that will get coverage.

It may be news that a candidate thinks or says we should take some drastic step to reduce energy consumption, but that is not television news unless he does it in a way that makes a spectacle out of it. Perhaps he might pour the gasoline out of his automobile into gallon jugs and give it away to people if they would agree not to waste it. That might get television coverage. The whole campaign has become structured in an effort to create a spectacle that the media will pay attention to, and the spectacle normally has to be no longer than a minute and a half, because anything longer than that exceeds the limits that the television spectacle people think is appropriate. They have to talk a little about it and explain why it is important, and about a minute and a half is normally the maximum. You might get more but you can not count on it. Good candidates learn to talk in thirty second intervals. And once you are doing it you sort of naturally fall into the habit. You know how to make a thirty second sentence so they can cut it there. Then you make another thirty second sentence so they can cut that. Give TV a choice of three bits to use, and if they have not got time for a minute and a half they can make a minute out of it without making it look awkward.

That is news or free coverage. Commercials or paid coverage are worse. Most candidates really do not like making thirty second and one minute commercials. I mean most of them really find it hard to take a complicated idea and compress it into thirty seconds or one minute. It is very difficult to do. Most candidates would really like to talk. They would like to have five minutes. And most candidates like to talk anyway. But you cannot buy five minutes. You cannot buy five minutes from television because the television networks have structured their day so that most programs run twenty-nine minutes or twenty-nine minutes and thirty seconds. They do not run 25 minutes. So how are you going to get five minutes out of that air time? The good media people work very hard to line up five-minute spots but most of them just abandon the idea. So that forces us into the one minute and thirty second commercial. And that is where this new art form has emerged and some of them are good and some of them are dreadful. Some of them are all image. Some of them have a kind of resonant substance behind them. But when you are through and done with it, they are all image; they are supposed to communicate to the voter an image of the kind of candidate the voter wants to see.

Now what has all this done to us? What it has done is created a smaller and smaller voting electorate every year since television became the dominant political instrumentality. And again the causes for that are fairly complicated and not easily laid out. They have a lot to do with Vietnam. They have a lot to do with a younger generation. They have a lot to do with a pretty dreadful educational system that has abandoned the notion that it is useful to teach children anything about government or American history. A whole generation has grown up without being exposed to the kind of things that some of us were exposed to. When I got back from World War II the most important thing to me was that I was now old enough to vote. But that is all gone.

We took a poll in the city of Hartford this year to find out why people do not vote. We picked Hartford because it had a mayoral election in November and if you wait a year to ask people whether they voted you will not get a truthful answer. They forget. They think they did. So if you want to poll non-voters you have got to do it the day after election day. We did, and the results were surprising. I had thought that the reason people were not voting was that they were angry, they were disillusioned, they were anti-government, they were loaded with negative feelings about politicians and politics. That turned out not to be true. The negative feelings they had about politics and government were quite similar to the negative feelings that the voters had about politics and government.

The big difference was age. We found that in Hartford about 20-22 percent of the population voted in that municipal election. We found that only 10 percent of those under thirty-five voted and 90 percent did not. We had expected that we would find a slow buildup from eighteen to twenty-four as people began to vote. But there is no statistical difference between the percentage of voters in the eighteen to twenty-four year group and the twenty-five to thirty-four year group.

What we concluded was that first of all nobody was addressing themselves to anything that would interest that generation. And secondly they had never acquired the habit of voting. But we also learned that they had about the same exposure to the campaign by way of television as the voters did. I think 91 percent or 92 percent of the voters said they got their information about the election from television and I think it was 89 percent of the non-voters got the information from the same source. The big difference was that the voters were older, the voters had some personal contact with the candidates—that is non-television contact—and the voters had received more literature, printed material, than the non-voters.

What this leads to is a peculiar kind of politics in which special interests have a tremendous opportunity to affect and control government. If you have a voting population of only 19 percent of the total population and you have special interests which can command 10 percent of the voters and that 10 percent actually turns out to vote, their special interest candidate will win. Now this is a theoretical model, but about four weeks ago the Alaska Republican Party had a series of caucuses to pick its party officials and the committees who will pick the Alaska Republican party candidates. On the night of the caucuses a group of Protestant fundamentalists turned out in unexpected numbers while everybody else stayed home. The next day the Alaska Republican party was the property of a group of Protestant Fundamentalists.

There are other examples. In 1968 we had a Senator Clark in Iowa, generally regarded as one of the better senators in the United States Senate. There was a low turnout election, somewhere around 32 percent, and in the course of his campaign he had somehow alienated the anti-abortion people and the gun lobby. So the gun lobby and the right-to-life people got together and mounted a campaign and they beat him. The possibilities for this are limitless.

You can see it in the 1980 Republican platform where the concentration among the delegates of the right-to-life, anti-abortion group and the anti-ERA group produced a platform result that is so inconsistent with every survey of public opinion on these issues that one can only say that the Republican party has not yet lost its capacity to commit suicide. But the reason for it is that the people who got themselves to be delegates represent special interests and were elected in low-turn-out elections.

A second consequence of all this is even worse. We tend to elect people who know how to campaign. The qualification to get elected is how good a performer you are. Not what do you know about government or what have you governed or your governmental record. They are rarely referred to. During this year's presidential mish-mash, the first time anybody made a serious study of Ronald Reagan's record as Governor of California was about three weeks after he had the nomination all wrapped up.

Why is Reagan the candidate? He is a superb performer. And he learned how to perform. Why was Carter the candidate in 1976? He was a superb performer. Now that is fine. If you want to be elected you ought to learn how to perform. But the problem is that television does not communicate any more than image and no one has figured out how to communicate the actuality of the capacity to govern. All that can be done is to create the image; the image can be created by a good image creator.

I think that if you look carefully at the record of the present administration in the last year you will see many, many examples of this and if you do what Professor Hans Eisle did out in Chicago—look at the polls that the president's pollster, Pat Cadell, conducted and then compare Cadell's reports with Carter's next speech—you find an incredible correlation. Eisle is critical because he does not think the questions were well put. But last year Carter's policy switches from a balanced budget to a non-balanced budget to a balanced budget; from tax cuts to no tax cuts to tax cuts—they are correlated remarkably to what the public opinion polls have reflected. Thus the pollster becomes more and more the formulator of public policy.

I do not know where we are headed in all this because it seems to me sooner or later there has to be a reaction to it. I can give you an example of a reaction which may happen this year.

If you want to define issues that might move the eighteen to thirty-four year-old population to get interested in government, I can think of a couple. That eighteen to thirty-four generation honest-to-God does not believe that there should be differences between men and women as far as their legal rights are concerned. That young generation has grown up believing in a system of equality between sexes, and they live it. Tell them that people—that men and women—are not equal and the federal government is not going to back up that proposition and you are going to stir them up.

But go a step further and tell them that abortion is going to be unconstitutional. This generation has grown up in an entirely different kind of world than Mr. Reagan did or Mr. Carter did. This is an issue that can generate a reaction among this age group. And if it turns out that instead of 20 percent of it voting there is 60 percent or 70 percent of it voting, you will turn the whole electoral process upside down. I anticipate that something like that is going to happen down the road and we are going to reactivate the electorate.

One other way to do it, and Carter almost stumbled into this, was to have a registration or a draft of everybody between twenty and thirty-four. But his pollster was very smart. He figured out that the nineteen and twenty year olds were isolated enough and just between high school and college and would not react and respond at the ballot box and there were too few of them anyway, so they limited the registration to nineteen and twenty year olds—as if we are going to build an army consisting of only nineteen and twenty year olds.

As for the future of the political system: it really comes down to a question of whether or not our political process is going to be, and continue to be, dominated by our technology or whether or not somehow out of all this a political system will emerge which uses the new technology but is not controlled by it. If I were to take a quick look today I really would have to say that our political process is dominated by our technology, that no one is really in control of that technology except the technicians, that they are not really quite sure what power they have in their hands although they are a little nervous about it, and that we are probably at a watershed which will determine whether or not we continue to run our government by projecting images and hoping that somehow out of it all someone will emerge who knows something about the governmental process.

McGARRY: Listening to Mr. Costikyan talk about the electronic media and its important role in American elections called to mind a story that really brought that home to me with a tremendous impact. I was in Beverly Hills, California when Ronald Reagan, who had never held an elective office, was aspiring to run for Governor of California. A gentleman and I were sitting in his den having a drink, and he said, "There is a TV program on this evening we must see—Ronald Reagan is launching his campaign. It is really a colossal joke." Now this gentleman was a very liberal Democrat and I assumed that he just had a built-in resentment against a conservative Republican. "Can you imagine this movie star running for Governor," he said. "I wouldn't mind if he ran for local assemblyman, or school commission or something, but he says he wants to become Governor of California!" And so we sat there listening to Reagan, and about 15 or 20 minutes into the program I noticed the gentleman was getting mesmerized and he couldn't take his eyes off the screen. He was silent and he was glued to the set.

Well Mr. Reagan had many years of marvelous experience before the camera and he was a natural on television. At the end of that program my companion banged his fist on the little table and the drink jumped up and he says, "I'll be a son-of-a-gun he makes a lot of sense." Well I left and came back to Boston not thinking much of the California election until I read that Mr. Reagan had won overwhelmingly. Reagan's win was not a matter of timing. Reagan took on the incumbent Governor, a real giant, and he knocked him off. So I agree with Mr. Costikyan's observation that the electronic media really dominate our electoral process in the United States, and that 90 percent of any campaign fund goes into the electronic media which brings us to money, and I do not think anybody quarrels with the proposition that money is the mother's milk of politics.

I am from the Federal Election Commission. It is a fairly new bureaucracy, only been in existence for five years. I do not think anybody would question the fact that it resulted from the infamous Watergate scandal. But the Watergate scandal did not put on the books the most dramatic election reform legislation in the history of this country. That election reform was precipitated by the skyrocketing cost of elections. In the 1968 election Richard Nixon and the late Hubert Humphrey spent about $40 million—Nixon $25 million and Humphrey about $15 million—and that was a shock.

Nixon and McGovern in 1972 spent about $62 million, most of it by Nixon. But the new reform law went on the books in 1972 and took effect right in the middle of the election campaign. As a matter of fact Nixon's finance chairman, Maurice Stans, was running around the country because the law was to take effect on April 8th and all you had to show on that date was your opening cash balance. So there was a mad scramble to get as much money in before they had to indicate where the money came from.

In the two days before the law became effective, Richard Nixon raised $6 million and $1.5 of it was in cash. And all they had to show as of April 8th was the opening cash balance. But as of that date the name of the game became disclosure. And the new law is now rigidly enforced.

In any event when you are talking about the work of the Federal Election Commission you really have three considerations: public financing, limitation on contributions, and disclosure.

The public financing aspect of the system comes down to money for primaries and money for the general election. The nominees of the opposing parties get $29.4 million each, as a grant. And they cannot raise any private money.

For example, four years ago President Carter, after he had been nominated, had lunch at "21" with two gentlemen— Mr. Bronfman of the Seagram Whiskey Corporation and Mr. Austin of Coca Cola for the purpose of introducing Mr. Carter to the business community in New York. The two gentlemen picked up the check, and they were stunned to find out four days later that they had violated the law, that the luncheon was viewed as a contribution and that the candidate accepting the general grant of money in the general election could not take any contributions. Ultimately the two hosts paid civil penalties, fines; and Mr. Carter had to return the cost of the luncheon to the Federal Treasury in the form of a fine.

Simply stated, if you were a citizen of the United States and decided to run for President of the United States, you could begin to get public money by raising a minimum of $100,000 comprised of no less than $5,000 in contributions from 20 different states, with contributions of no more than $250 from any one individual. After that the federal treasury will give you matching money. Your threshold requirement is raising $5,000 in 20 states with contributions of not more than $250 per individual, so that no one person can give you the $5,000. You have to have a minimum of 50 people, and 20 states. And that qualifies you. With that you have $100,000.

Now you can run without the public money. You do not have to take the public money. But if you take the public money you must agree in writing that you will observe limitations and that you will keep records and make your books available for a mandatory audit by government auditors who really do a very thorough, comprehensive audit of all your books. With that agreement you ultimately can raise and get matching money up to $5 million.

Finally we should note that the federal government finances the conventions and the campaigns. They are going to give the

Democratic and the Republican Conventions $4.4 million each; and each candidate will get $29.4 million. And in brief, those are the essentials of public financing.

IV

The Nominating Process: Primaries and Delegate Selection

Gerald M. Pomper
Miriam Bockman

POMPER: The Presidential nominating system has gone through four different stages. These represent not just historical changes but four different theories of what parties should be and how officials, particularly the President, should be elected.

The first stage, which ought to be familiar to Europeans is conceiving of a party as a group of parliamentary leaders or notables, with the party leader as the person chosen by his colleagues in the national legislature. That was the original American system; it existed for roughly a quarter of a century, in which the party members in Congress would get together and select a candidate for president. That was the so-called "congressional caucus system," and I emphasize that it is still used essentially in most European countries where the leader of the party is also its parliamentary leader.

But that system decayed, broke down for various reasons, we got to a second stage and a second theory of what a party is: namely that a party was conceived to be a coalition of state and local parties, and of different groups associated with them, that come together, usually only every four years, to bargain among themselves and to choose the leader. Obviously this was a decentralized process compared to the previous system, a very different system, a very different belief in what a party is.

That system worked reasonably well for over a century, roughly 1836-1948, and it is from that period that most of the interesting stories and legends about American politics come. Conventions sometimes would go on as long as two and a half weeks. The longest convention ever was held in New York City in 1924. American humorist Will Rogers said that the convention had to come to an end because the delegates needed a bath and they could not get a decent one in New York. Most of the time they were shorter than that but there was a good deal of bargaining, compromising, dealing; exchanges were made during that time and we got some fairly good candidates out of it, some terrible ones as well, but many interesting stories.

My favorite is of the 1932 Democratic Convention when Franklin Roosevelt came without the clear majority he needed. He finally made a deal with the manager for another candidate who then became vice president. The deal was sealed at a hotdog stand where the two candidates' managers were eating hotdogs and the final line of the deal was, "Okay we will settle this in the morning and please pass the mustard." Thus out of such basic materials as hotdogs and mustard, came Roosevelt and the New Deal.

Well, for any number of reasons that system too had its defects and began to collapse in 1952, which not coincidentally was the first year in which television was a major influence on American politics. We evolved to what I still regard as the best system for presidential nominations, which for want of a better term, I am calling here the "mixed system." A system in which state party leaders and some national party leaders still had an important influence, decisions still would be made through their bargaining but they did not have unlimited discretion. They had to pay a great deal of attention to indicators of popular support. The candidates would go out into the states, contest some primaries, usually no more than about half a dozen to prove that they had some popular support, that they could campaign, that they could finally win the election.

The purpose of that campaigning was not really to win those delegates in the state primary. The purpose was to prove to the party leaders that they could eventually win an election. So there was a mixture here of appealing to the voters but, as well, ultimately appealing to the party leaders. And it was through that kind of combination that Dwight Eisenhower was nominated in 1952 and John Kennedy in 1960. Both of whom I think are models of how the system can work to give you both party support and popular support.

Finally we come to the present system in which we have a new theory of party. Parties are not seen as groups of notables or as coalitions of different factions, but although no one has said this explicitly—are essentially seen as mass movements. The party is seen as some kind of elemental democratic combination of individuals. There should not be, there is no legitimacy for, intermediate groups; or for strong party leaders. Somehow a party is supposed to be an almost spontaneous gathering of individuals who should directly decide on important party decisions, the most important of course being the nomination of a presidential candidate.

And so we have moved only in the last three nominations, 1972, 1976 and 1980 to this theory of the party as a collection of individual members directly choosing presidential candidates. And we will come back to this later when we talk about the quality, the merits and defects of this system. Now let me talk about the formal rules of how delegates are selected.

The organizing idea of the formal rules, is really a combination of two principles: the first one is federalism; the second is national choice. The United States of course is a federal nation in which the 50 states and a couple of territories are viewed as independent political units for some purposes; the nominating system and delegate selection system recognize that federal quality. It is mixed, though with a very different aspect—the national presidency. For the president will be selected by the entire country. The present system attempts to meld these two ideas of direct popular control and selection with the existence of the subordinate political units of a federal system.

This attempt shows up, for example, in the way delegates are allocated among the states and you may wonder about this—why does California have 280 delegates and New Jersey only 90 and so on? The principle by which the delegates are distributed among the states differs in the two parties.

The Democratic party theory is essentially one of voter individualism. The delegates should be distributed among the states because of the number of people that exist in those states. But the people in the states are counted in two different ways. They are counted first on the basis of population: how many individuals are there in each state. But second of all they are counted on the basis of how many Democrats there are in those states and that of course is not the same thing.

The Democratic party uses a complicated formula essentially giving half the delegates to the state on the basis of population and half the delegates on the basis of how many Democratic votes are there in that state.

The Republican party leans more toward the federal system, allocating delegates first on the basis of how many congressmen exist in the states, and then adding a certain number of extra or bonus votes to each state. If the state voted for a Republican candidate for president last time it gets more delegates. If it voted for a Republican candidate for senator it gets more delegates, and so on through a number of offices. So it takes the basic principle of federalism and adds to it on the basis of how the state has done for the Republican party.

This system produces a large number of delegates—approximately 3000 for the Democratic party, 2000 for the Republicans—but it is impossible for that number of delegates to really make a rational decision, if it were left up to them. Tom Wicker in the New York Times, in an article surely inspired by the Kennedy campaign, suggests that the delegates really ought to deliberate and ought to make rational decisions. Well two or three thousand people cannot possibly deliberate and conduct any kind of real decision making, so this is a naive argument.

The delegates get to the conventions through two different methods with basic similarities. The first method is the caucus system. Caucuses are simply party meetings to which any member of the party can come and ask to be a delegate. Now this works in a very homey kind of way, beginning at a very local level. People in an area no larger than a county will be invited to come to an open meeting, publicized in advance. Anyone who wants to come can come to this meeting and say, "I would like to be a delegate."

A local caucus may actually start below the county level, where delegates might be chosen for a county caucus. Then county delegates might get together and choose delegates for a congressional district caucus, and people could meet there and choose delegates for the state caucus; finally at the state caucus delegates to the national convention would be chosen. So it is a multi-stage process that eventually brings a small number of people to the convention itself.

To give you an example: I attended the caucus in my home county, Middlesex County, New Jersey. It was open to anybody;

you could bring friends if you wanted to be a delegate. I didn't bring enough friends, so I did not get to be a delegate, but other people did. Now the problem is that very few people will come to a caucus in a county which has 6000 people, 100 people came to the caucus I am describing, so it is quite likely that you are going to get a strange distribution of delegates selected.

In my particular caucus, a Democratic caucus, eight delegates were to be chosen, and the result was they named three blacks, two Puerto Ricans, one feminist, one labor union official and one homosexual—quite a diverse crew. But in a county at least 60 percent Catholic, only one of those eight candidates was Catholic. In an area in which Rutgers University, here I teach, is a major element and a major population group, nobody from the university was chosen.

It was a very strange kind of selection process, and perhaps the strangest, I might even say "queerest" element was that the final decision on the last two delegates to be chosen was arrived at by a deal between different factions. That of course is typical in politics, but the deal was made between the homosexual on the one hand and the labor union official on the other. Each would vote for the other in order to get nominated. A very strange alliance, but as you know politics makes strange bedfellows.

Twenty-five percent of the delegates are now chosen through the caucus method. The other three-quarters are chosen through state primaries, and that is a major change. As recently as 1968 only about 25 percent were chosen through state primaries, the rest were chosen through caucuses and party methods. So we have had a complete reversal of these proportions.

The primary system has enormous variations to it. But the major point is that virtually none of them, no two of the 36 primaries, are the same. Every state sets its own laws, subject to certain general party regulations, and they are all very different.

There are some principles that run through them now. One that is critical, especially in the Democratic party is that when voters go to the polls to vote in the state primary for the delegates to the national convention, the delegates that are chosen have to be chosen in proportion to the preferences of the voters. That is, if

30 percent of the voters prefer Kennedy and say so on the ballot, 30 percent of the delegates chosen must be Kennedy delegates. If 60 percent of them prefer Carter, 60 percent of the delegates must be Carter delegates.

That principle is very rigidly adhered to in the Democratic party now. It is less rigidly adhered to in the Republican party, but still the trend is in that direction.

The principle of proportionality is now carried down not only to the state level—30 percent for Reagan in the state, 30 percent of the delegates must be for Reagan—but to the district level. Especially in the Democratic party, delegates are chosen in smaller districts than the state and those delegates must be proportionally divided.

So if an individual district, usually a congressional district, elects three delegates, and Reagan gets 30 percent of the vote, he would get one delegate, one-third of the representation. This is proportional representation at the lowest possible level.

Another characteristic of the primary system is that people who want to be delegates generally indicate which presidential candidate they are for and the voters vote for that delegate not because they want the delegate, but because they want a certain individual to be president. There again, the tie is very close. What the voter wants is what the delegates should do and is what the convention should do. Regardless of what Tom Wicker says, people often do not even know the delegate's name, they vote for the delegate because they want a certain person for president.

Certain technical provisions are also important. Most important is the designation of slates. For the most part delegates do not run as individuals but on a slate pledged to Carter, Kennedy, Reagan, Bush, whomever, and that pledge is enforcable probably by the courts and certainly enforceable by the conventions themselves. An important thing that is happening in the Democratic party now is movement toward a rule saying that a delegate must vote for the candidate he indicated he favored. He has no discretion and he is simply a counting device on behalf of his presidential candidate.

Well what are the effects of these rules? Three vital ones. The entire process first of all is dominated by candidates. The candidates organize this process; the candidates enter the state primaries;

the candidates use the delegate slates; the candidates conduct the campaign, spend the money, buy the television time, and ultimately it is the candidates who are named in the public opinion polls. This very organized process is coordinated by the candidates in an individualistic system—perhaps too individualistic and not organized by parties, as it once was.

There were always of course candidates running for president, but they ran for president by getting parties, particularly during the long period of party dominance, state parties, to support them. Now candidates go directly to the voters and they try to organize and win their support. They try to bring people out to caucuses, they try to bring them out to primaries, and so on.

The second characteristic and effect of these formal rules is that you get voter mandates. Voters can decide who will be president, although by no means is this a national kind of determination. Fewer than half the voters vote in these primaries. Fewer than half of those who are eligible, and in some states even lower than that. In my own state of New Jersey, which voted in June for president, 22 percent of the eligible voters voted in the primary. The voter mandate as to who should be president, collected in individual states, is a mandate by a minority, tending to be more ideologically concerned, more upper class in character and so on.

The most important effect of these rules—I keep repeating this but it is decisive—is that the party as an organized group is simply excluded from the process. The national party has always been excluded from this and now state parties and local parties have very little to do with it as well.

Let me deal now with the candidates, who come in a number of varieties. One special kind of candidate is an incumbent president, whether it is Gerald Ford in 1976 or Jimmy Carter in 1980. They typically follow a strategy of appearing to be very presidential, the "Rose Garden Strategy." It means the president stays in the rose garden of the White House and runs for president from there.

More important than staying in the White House though, is the power of the presidency. There's an enormous amount of discretion that presidents have in using federal money, federal favors and so on which can influence the way people vote. The man in charge of trying to win Florida for President Carter this year told me about his campaign, saying, "They did not use federal money crassly. They did not go down and say, 'If you vote, if your county votes for Carter, we will give you so much money.' But they used it subtly. Places where they had support got quicker consideration for their needs for new money for highways or for schools or for transportation and so on." In fact he said he went down to Florida with $200 million in federal grants to give out. And that has helped the president a good deal.

A different kind of candidate is a candidate who begins a presidential year as the most obvious candidate, the so-called "front-runner." Sometimes they succeed, sometimes they run into trouble. Ronald Reagan began as a front-runner, essentially maintained that position during the first three months of this year, and by that time had won the nomination in all but formal terms.

Sometimes they do not succeed. Edmund Muskie ran for president in 1972 and everybody said he was sure to be the nominee, but he ran into a number of problems and left the race by the month of March and went back to the Senate.

The most interesting races are ones in which there are multiple candidates who try successively to eliminate one another.

Beyond candidates there are other participants. Financiers are critical. They put up the money for campaigns, which used to be essentially a private operation. Sometimes you could find one "angel" to give you $2 million. Nixon had such a person and that led to problems, Watergate in particular. Now most of the money for nominations comes through federal matching grants. For every dollar a candidate can raise, the federal government will give another dollar, with certain limitations. In turn the candidate agrees not to spend more than a certain amount of money.

The maximum this year is $17.5 million, which sounds like a lot of money but actually works out to less than 50¢ per voter in the primaries. And it is very tough to run primary campaigns with so little money, particularly in an inflationary period. Especially when inflation has affected campaign spending more than it has affected other things. The general inflation rate over the last four years has been 35 percent which is bad enough. In terms of airplane charters, which candidates use, it has been 145 percent and the candidates have to pay for those airplanes. The cost of television advertising has risen something like 67 percent, again more than the rate of general inflation. So it is tough to run a campaign. Particularly tough because you cannot get money from private individuals in amounts greater than $1000 per person. That limitation was set for the 1976 election, but in 1980 $1000 is only worth $740. So you are trying to buy more expensive material with no more money. Money is a crucial matter and becomes a very hard limitation on campaigns.

Another major participant is the mass media and the opinion polls connected to it. Much of the campaign has to be conducted through television, because it is impossible to meet many voters any other way. The impression that one makes on television, and even more the impression one makes on television commentators is critically important. Instead of parties now deciding who is a likely candidate, television commentators and the press generally make this decision.

There is a process of candidate elimination that goes on even before the election year begins in which the press, not through some conspiracy but simply by talking to one another, decide who the likely candidates are and simply eliminate some people from consideration while advancing others. I have a great deal of respect for John Anderson, but I think his candidacy owes a lot to the fact that television and the press seem to love him. He gets enormous amounts of press attention and favorable commentary.

On the other hand the press decided that Howard Baker probably did not have much of a chance. Although he has been a tremendously effective legislator, he never got the kind of attention that might have made him a more important presidential candidate. Consider the Roger Mudd interview with Ted Kennedy. Now I do not think that was a good performance by Ted Kennedy, and I do not know the ratings it got, but I venture to say that only a relatively small minority of the electorate saw that interview and felt that Ted Kennedy did badly. Far more important, in my opinion, is that all the commentators *said* Ted Kennedy did terribly in this interview. They said, "He really does not have the qualities of a presidential candidate." If you hear that often enough, you assume it must be true.

The same thing with the TV debate between Nixon and Kennedy in 1960. Although this was not for the nomination but the election. Nixon did do badly in that debate; even the people who saw the debate said that. But the people who did not see the debate were even more convinced that Nixon did badly than those who saw it. And there were secondary effects: "Nixon must be terrible, he did so badly in the debate." "Did you see it?" "No, but Roger Mudd or Walter Cronkite or somebody told me he did badly." And so the television and the press generally have become major participants in the process.

We still have state and local parties, interest groups, voting blocs, and candidate groups and so on, and they too are important. The strategies that come out of this fact are four: Early organization is critical because the campaign has become a widespread one in which you need to win delegates throughout the nation, and because of the proportional representation system in which you can go anywhere and hope for a few delegates, even in enemy territory. In this system the advantage goes to somebody who organizes early, who has diffuse support and who has nothing else to do but campaign. It is interesting and I think significant that the last two nominations of people who were not incumbent presidents went to an unemployed former governor of Georgia, who had nothing else to do but run around campaigning, and in 1980 to an unemployed former governor of California. This system makes it more difficult for somebody who has a fulltime job to run for president because he does not have the same time to organize in all these states and to meet people by the hundreds and thousands.

The second strategy that becomes important is getting a favorable interpretation of what has happened. Any state primary can be read in very different ways. To get your interpretation accepted, especially by television, is critical. My favorite example is Jimmy Carter, unknown at the beginning of 1976 but vigorously campaigning in Iowa and then New Hampshire. In the New Hampshire primary Carter got the grand total of 22,000 votes—not a heck of a lot of votes—28 percent of the total vote. 28 percent. Television decided that Carter had won the primary. Though he did come in first, 28 percent is not very good. But television decided he won. *Time* magazine put him on its front cover—that is 29 million copies every week going into the homes of Americans—and he was declared to be the front-runner on the basis of winning fewer than 30,000 votes in a small and not terribly representative state.

Being declared the front-runner leads in turn to other things. To more money. People start contributing more to you and the money is doubled. Every dollar you collect from an individual, the federal government matches. It leads to a better position in public opinion polls. That in turn leads to more television attention, which in turn leads to more money and a better position in the television polls. And what you get of course is a cycle developing momentum, as the cliché has it, like a snowball rolling down a hill and gathering more and more snow as it goes along.

A related strategy is ideological dominance. Particularly in a nomination in which there are many people representing the same wing of the party. A critical part of the strategy is to get rid of other people like yourself. If you are conservative, get rid of the other conservative. Reagan did that very well. The other conservatives were John Connally and Philip Crane, who lost to him and dropped out quickly. If you can reduce the race ultimately to your ideological wing against the other, then you have a fairly good chance. George Bush's problem was that he was trying to do exactly that, to be seen as the only moderate candidate against the conservative Reagan. The problem is nobody believed him. Anderson stayed too long. By the time Bush was the only candidate of the moderate left, Reagan already had too large a number of delegates.

This all leads finally to the last strategy: momentum. Keep building up more support through the primaries, the polls and financing, leading to more support in primaries and eventually to the nomination. This system first of all stresses individual candidates. If you had the time and the inexhaustible patience to watch television coverage and even newspaper coverage of a campaign, you would find an incredible stress on individual characteristics, personalities and the race itself.

Television spends most of its time, and there are detailed studies on this, asking who is ahead? It spends very little time asking what is this candidate like? Is he honest? Does he beat his wife? Does he run away from disasters? Most of the time they spend on who is ahead in the race, which is a kind of meta-television. Television examining itself and what it is supposed to be covering, with almost no time at all spent on what the candidates believe in, their issue positions and so on, except as those issues affect who is ahead.

Parties are subordinated in this process—eliminated would probably not be too strong a word—and a third result is very early decisions. We have seen this now two or three convention years running. I think it is built into the system of finance; it is built into the system of polling; and it is built into the system of television coverage wanting desperately to know who is going to win. The prediction of who is going to win becomes a self-confirming one. If everybody believes Reagan will be the nominee, the voters are less likely to try and prevent that from happening, as we saw in this year's primary voting. Once the early primaries were over, participation dropped enormously. People did not believe it mattered and so there was less attempt to choose a different candidate.

Do we have a good system? I suggest five standards for evaluating the choice. Commentators have never believed the system could work. Walter Bagehot, the great English commentator and social scientist, talked about the nomination of Abraham Lincoln in 1860, and he was just aghast at it. Here were midnight conferences among drunken politicians, corrupt deals—there were some wonderfully corrupt deals in 1860—people in a frenzy, not knowing what to do. And somehow you get Abraham Lincoln out of it. Bagehot thought it had to be the hand of God. It certainly could not be anything inherent in the system.

So we need some standards for evaluation. I think any nation benefits if its choice of candidates is a wide choice. If we are not restricted to just one kind of person for president but can go into different areas and different kinds of persons. The present system has some qualities like that. A wide choice exists in the sense that you are not limited to professional politicians, you are not limited to parliamentary leaders. People with different backgrounds can run for president. There is something admirable about a system that does make it possible for an obscure governor from Georgia to become a presidential candidate.

This is balanced by other problems. The matter of full consideration. We begin with a wide choice of candidates. It is true in some ways that almost anybody can run for president, and after Jimmy Carter I think you can say almost anybody can be president. But it is not full consideration in the sense of timeliness. The process works to reach a decision very early. March or April of the election year seems to be about the outside time when a presidential candidate is going to be chosen. A two-person race like Ford-Reagan in 1976 may be a different situation. But that limits the choice people have because it means that new thoughts, new considerations, new weaknesses, and new outside events are not going to have any kind of effect. Jimmy Carter in 1976 had wrapped up the nomination by the middle of April. In May and June he kept losing primaries. He showed a great deal of weakness and yet there was no way to reverse that earlier decision.

Later events do not affect the convention. The decision has already been made and so we begin with a wide choice of candidates which is good, but we close that decision very quickly which I think is bad in terms of the process, regardless of the candidates who actually get nominated.

Another criterion that I would use is, does the process select candidates who are not only popular—and a president has to have popular support—but also politically skilled; who have the ability to bargain with other politicians, to coerce them if necessary, to deal with Congress, and so on.

I think this process does give us candidates who have some kind of popular appeal. After all that is how they win the nomination, by getting votes in primary. But it undercuts, it deemphasizes, the ability to deal with other politicians and I think Carter is not an accidental but a perfect example of this. The defects that Carter has shown, the problems that he has had with Congress, in negotiating with other politicians, are in part attributable to the fact that he never had to prove his ability to bargain with other politicians in getting nomination. A Franklin Roosevelt kind of nomination was a test of that ability. In order to become president, Roosevelt had to deal with other politicians and that gave you an indication that when it came to being president, he could deal with other politicians in Congress as well. The present system does not ensure that.

The fourth standard to note is party unity and party continuity. Does the process help a party to become unified, does it help the party maintain its historical continuity—to previous candidates, to previous positions, to its previous record? The present system does not do that very well, as the party has been eliminated as an independent influence. You can get candidates who do not represent the party as such, who do not stand on its historic record, and who do not necessarily unify it as a party. I am not completely sure of this, but certainly the process leaves nominations open to individual candidates who do not represent the historical continuity of the party. It is entirely possible, to be wildly speculative, that if George Wallace had not been shot, and we had the full development of this system in 1972, that Wallace would have been the Democratic candidate for president. He got more votes in the primaries than any other candidate, including George McGovern, and if he had had more primaries to go into, he might have been the candidate. Whatever else one might say about George Wallace, he certainly did not represent the historical continuity of the Democratic party and yet he might have been the party's candidate.

The final criterion I would use is system legitimacy. Does the process have basic support in the country as a proper way to choose a presidential candidate? The old system, the convention system, lost that legitimacy. I guess it lost it in the streets of Chicago in 1968. The present system, strange as it seems, probably does have popular legitimacy and that makes it very difficult to change and to go back to revise in any substantial way. That may be its greatest strength. People think it is good and they might even want it to go further.

BOCKMAN: I think the main thing that has been taken away from presidential convention delegates and perhaps from the public at large is the fun. After all a delegate used to be able to go to a convention and feel that he or she—in those days it was mostly he—would at least be dealt with in some way and have a substantive role to play. That role now has been relegated to such matters as a fight on rules for that particular convention or for future conventions, party rules, platform fights, credentials fights, things that do not have very much to do with the selection of the president. That has already been done. It is true, however, that the credibility of the procedure, something which the people in my wing of the Democratic party, the reformers, have been fighting for, is greater in the sense that the individual voter has more to say about who the candidate will be. And perhaps in the not too distant future we may even eliminate the conventions and select a candidate strictly through primary procedure.

Now the process is essentially a contest of let us try to pick the winner and pick the winner early because what we really want to do is be in a good position in the future to have access, not only to the White House, but to the enormous structure of the federal government whence all benefits derive. And that is very important not just in the sense that you want political favors, but if anybody is interested in receiving benefits from the federal government, they have to in some way be able to have access to the various agencies and to people in the White House in order to expedite that process and to see that they at least get what they perceive as fair for themselves. Whether that involves getting money for our schools or jobs for our people, you need access.

So there is that kind of foot shuffling and thinking and conversations that go on especially in the earlier parts of a campaign. How do you deliver that initial primary vote? What help do you give to the candidates that you choose and so on?

In the delegate selection process itself, at least as it applies to New York State, the Republican delegates are still chosen by a method which does not identify them on the ballot as being committed to any candidate.

But the people who ran for delegate in the Democratic party had to sign a commitment that they would indeed vote on the first ballot for the candidate that they were representing.

But only the first ballot. You might have a situation where no one has a clear majority going in and in that case the second ballot would become the one where the old fashioned methods would then come into play once again. However, there has not been a second ballot in a convention since 1952. And that is largely because the new system, with all the media attention and with the amounts of money that people haved to commit, has made it pretty much impossible.

With regard to the media it should be noted that it is not just who they think is winning or who they like and want to give attention to, there is also the very human aspect of what is good professionally, of asking, "What is going to give us the most interesting thing to talk about during these months preceding a convention? How can we keep the interest of our reader or our watcher?"

For example, at one point in the '79-80 campaign, it looked as though Kennedy was going to be the leader in the Democratic party. Carter did not have a chance. Till the Roger Mudd interview. As soon as Kennedy was officially in the race, he became a target and had to be erased, and if you look at headlines of the time or you look at the television news broadcasts of the time, you will find a decided tendency to attack and make Senator Kennedy a target. This coincided with the beginning of the Iranian crisis and then with Afghanistan, which created a lot of support for Carter, and so the perception of the electorate began to change.

Then, after the Iowa primary, at the end of January, when it looked like Carter might just take off and go, you could look at the newspapers and see an immediate change again in the slant of the headlines. All of a sudden Carter, now the front runner, became the target and again it began to look as if it could be a race. I have discussed this with newspeople, and sometimes they allowed as to how it might be true that they were catering to self-interest in this kind of thing. But in any event they do make a big difference.

It is also worth noting that polling can be a double-edged sword. The American people very often look at a poll and say, "Oh so-and-so only got 10 percent, poor thing. Let us make him or her feel a little better." And you will find that there will be a switch in the next polls. It is totally emotional, it has nothing to do with whether they think the person is good, bad or indifferent, but is just a kind of let's-be-nice sort of thing. So the polls have an actual effect sometimes beyond just reporting. They actually create the next impact.

The Nominating Process: Primaries and Delegate Selection   69

I believe that the people should select the presidential candidates. We have tried to create that kind of scenario. But while trying to expand the base from which the presidential candidates are chosen, in some way we have also reduced that base because not everyone votes. Indeed the majority of voters come from certain parts of the population. They come from the better educated parts of the population, the more affluent parts of the population, and the effort to bring people into vote can sometimes be self-defeating.

It has been said that caucuses for instance were held in an area as small as a county. Well, as small as a county in New York state can be several hundred miles in every direction in an area with no public transportation, where in some of the early caucus months there may be heavy snows. So you will have a caucus such as the one in Middlesex County where 100 people show up, or as in a couple of caucuses where 15 people showed up in a county that has several hundred thousand people.

Or you could have the opposite in Manhattan where we have a density of population that includes two full congressional districts and two partial congressional districts. The caucuses were held by congressional districts; each of which has about 250,000 people. If we had had a reasonable turnout of the voters, 30 percent, there is no room—including Madison Square Garden, where we could have held those caucuses. None of us knew what was going to happen.

In one congressional district we could easily have had four or five thousand people. But as it happened we had about 1,200 people in one school separated into Kennedy voters and Carter voters and that was about as much as we could handle. If more people had come, I do not think we could have handled it. But that comes out to about one percent of the party. One percent! Now again, in choosing those delegates you are looking for control, whether you are a special interest group like the homosexuals or the Right-To-Life people or a party person—everyone wants their people to be the ones who win because even though those people no longer have anything to say, except about the rules or the platform, it is an indication of power.

Now if you say the people should choose and you should keep your hands off, remember that anyone who brings the right number of friends can win. But anybody who thinks about it more than 30 seconds knows that there will be groups getting together ahead of time, pulling their people in, making sure they are going to go, and that they can control a caucus very easily because they know very few people are coming.

So that is the caucus system. It leads someone like myself to question whether we are really reaching out in the best and the most democratic way.

V

The Nominating Process: Conventions

Rita W. Cooley
Basil A. Paterson

COOLEY: Here is a quotation about presidential elections from one of the most insightful tourists ever to visit our country, Alexis De Tocqueville:

For a long time before the appointed time is at hand the election becomes the most important and all-engrossing topic of discussion. The order of faction is doubled and all the artificial passions which the imagination can create in the bosom of a happy and peaceful land are agitated and brought to light. The President on the other hand is absorbed by the cares of self-defense. He no longer governs for the interest of the State but for that of reelection. He does homage to the majority and instead of checking its passions as his duty commands him to do, frequently courts its worst caprices. As the election draws near the activity of intrigue and the agitation of the populace increase, the citizens are divided into several camps each of which assumes the name of its favorite candidate, the whole nation glows with feverish excitement. The election is the daily theme of the papers, the subject of private conversation, the end of every thought and every action, the sole interest. As soon as the choice is determined, this order is dispelled. A calmer season returns. The current of the State which has nearly broken its banks, sinks to its usual level. But who can refrain from astonishment at the causes of the storm.

Choosing political leaders is a problem as old as society. In most democracies they are screened and developed through political parties. A British MP once said, "great leaders of parties are not elected, they are evolved. The leader is there and we all know it when he is there. Everybody who matters knows who the leader will be." Now, the formal procedures by which the major American parties pick their leaders is very far from that kind of system.

Our nominations are made in public, they are governed by the calendar, they are not confined to politicians, they are rule bound, and even non-members of parties participate in them. Historically, the convention emerged as a vehicle of nomination after political parties came on the scene and changed the original method of choosing a President presented in the Constitution, namely where notables from the various states—the Electoral College—would decide who the best man was. This is the manner in which George Washington, of course, was elected unanimously.

Now, political parties arrived rather early in the United States. They were clearly evident in the elections of 1796 and 1800, and the parties soon converted the Electoral College into what is tantamount to a popular electoral vote, with some possibility for slippage. The Constitution is absolutely silent on the question of nominations, and in fact the term political party is not used in the United States Constitution. So our system has had to evolve over the years.

The early method used was for leading figures in the Congress to nominate. But this Congressional caucus system broke down in 1824 when you had four men of the same political party running for the presidency, with the consequence that the election went to the House of Representatives. That led to the party convention system, and the national nominating convention has been the method used in this country since 1832, by both major and indeed minor parties as well.

Including all aspects of the process connected with it, this system is the most elaborate, complex, prolonged and exhausting system—both for the candidates and for the public—that the mind of man could conceive.

Now the longevity and general acceptance of the convention is in large part due to the multiplicity of functions which it uniquely performs. It is a nominating body, of course. But it also writes a platform presenting the party positions on campaign issues.

It serves as the supreme governing body, making major decisions on party affairs. It is a forum for compromise among diverse elements within the party, allowing for discussion and accomodation of different points of view. And it really is the ultimate campaign rally, gathering thousands of party leaders and rank and file members from across the country in one city.

What conventions are not, however, are super legislatures which have any capacity whatsoever for enforcing their policy views on the executive branch or particularly on the Congress. Members of the Congress are subject to different constituencies and different risks than convention delegates, so Congress is really free to ignore some of the pious statements that may be made in platforms at the National Convention.

We must distinguish the "old-style convention" from the present convention. The old-style convention was characterized by a lot of hoopla, a carnival atmosphere, hats, bands, which frequently masked very serious political issues and political divisions. The primary mode was one of bargaining and compromise among state political leaders, often called "kingmakers," who interacted with each other and with significant pressure groups.

The old system was characterized by "deals." To give a few historical examples: Lincoln's first nomination in 1860 was secured by a very complex deal made by his managers with all of his political rivals, of whom there were several, under which most of them ended up in his cabinet. In 1936 Franklin Delano Roosevelt needed Texas and California in order to put him over, and between the first and third ballots his managers, particularly Jim Farley, struck the necessary deals in order to give the votes of California and Texas to FDR. The price in that instance was the Vice Presidency— one of the currencies in which the kingmakers used to deal—and John Nance Garner, a politician from Texas, Speaker of the House of Representatives, became Roosevelt's first Vice President.

Democratic Conventions often used to be very lengthy, because of the old two-thirds rule, under which the President was nominated by a two-thirds vote of all the delegates.

This two-thirds rule effectively gave the South a veto. After the Civil War no one from the Deep South could be nominated, but through the operation of the two-thirds rule the Southerners were able to veto any candidate whom they did not approve. It also resulted in protracted, multiballot conventions.

Woodrow Wilson, for example, was nominated on the 46th ballot, in 1912. The all-time record is 103 ballots, when the Democratic delegates in 1924 finally came up with a dark horse compromise candidate after two major candidates knocked each other out. During that convention the satirist H.L. Mencken, wrote the following:

There is something about a national convention that makes it as fascinating as a revival or a hanging. It is vulgar, it is ugly, it is stupid, it is tedious, it is hard upon both the cerebral centers and the gluteus maximus, and yet it is somehow charming. One sits through long sessions wishing heartily that all the delegates were dead in Hell, and then suddenly there comes a show so gaudy, so hilarious, so melodramatic, so unimaginably exhilarating and preposterous that one lives a gorgeous year in an hour.

Now this is a literary view. Other observers of the convention system over the past century and a half have criticized its carnival atmosphere, the lack of decorum and taste that seems to characterize our conventions, but it was a traditional fixture of American politics. In any event the old style convention is really a thing of the past. The kingmakers, the leaders of state delegations sitting in smoke-filled rooms, are gone, because both parties—and particularly the Democrats—have over the past decade or so instituted changes in the fundamental character of the convention.

After the bitter 1968 Democratic convention in Chicago with its very noisy and strident confrontations among party leaders, delegates, city officials, the media, the street demonstrators and even the cops, a decade of reform began. The tone was set by the so-called McGovern-Fraser Commission, which recommended changes, and there have been two or three subsequent commissions. The now dominant philosophy is incorporated in this statement from the McGovern-Fraser Commission: "The delegation should fairly reflect division of preferences, expressed by those who participate in the Presidential nominating processes." The Democratic party was reshaped in terms of participation. And the dominant influence within the convention shifted from party elites, the old bosses, the old state leaders interacting with interest group leaders who formerly had decided nominations, to individual delegates, 75% of whom are now selected in primaries, and by those voters who choose to participate in local caucuses.

Now there are more amateurs at conventions. 84% of the people who attended the 1972 convention had never been to a convention before. More women, more minorities (although the emphasis has shifted from quotas to affirmative action under the Winograd

Commission rules) has meant a more limited role for professional politicians, state and local leaders. Many state governors will not even be at the 1980 conventions.

This has all been done in the name of fairness, openness and kindliness. For example, the selections must be made in the same calendar year as the convention and proportionally, no "winner take all" in the Democratic party any more. Formerly a person could get a plurality one more vote than anyone else in a statewide primary, and get all that state's votes. That is no longer true. The state's votes are now distributed among the contestants in proportion to their popular votes. And they are pledged delegates. Under the rule proposed by the Winograd Commission all delegates to the National Convention are bound to vote for the presidential candidate they have been elected to support for at least the first convention ballot, unless released in writing by the candidate. So much for the Democrats.

The Republicans have also made some reforms but of a more more modest nature. They have not in general followed the participant-oriented, structural-change path taken by the Democrats. What the Republican National Committee has emphasized is rather new services and support to state party organizations. They have greatly increased the staff of the Republican National Committee. Its budget has taken a quantum leap.

The National Republican Party considers itself a service agency for the 50 state parties. It makes efforts to recruit new candidates at the state and local level. But there has been a spillover from the Democratic reforms, because many of the states in their efforts to comply with Democratic requirements provided for primaries, and therefore they were available to the Republicans as well as to the Democrats. Also these reforms have been coupled with federal financing of presidential elections and primaries, as well as limitations on contributions and these things have affected both parties.

The consequences have been that we have a great increase in the number of primaries, of contestants, and in the size of the conventions; more personal organizations by the candidates less use of party officials and party machinery, more use of political consultants. The greater number of primaries lessens the independent impact of the convention. It magnifies the role of the media. It tends to divorce the national nomination from state and local politics. It has weakened national parties. It has added to other forces making for party decomposition.

And all these tendencies have reinforced each other. Candidates have found primaries to be an important political opportunity. The message is now start early, campaign in many states, do not depend on the power brokers, develop a strong personal organization. And all of this has affected both the Democratic and the Republican parties.

There are, however differences between them, not only in the way in which they select convention delegates, but in the demographic and ideological characteristics of those delegates. The Republicans tend, for example, to be more upper class. The average income of the delegates at the 1976 convention was $46,000. More businessmen and more Protestants are Republican. The Democrats have more Catholics, more Jews, more Trade Unionists. Both are comparable, however, in that the people who go to the convention on the Republican side are likely to be more conservative than their counterparts in the electorate at large, while on the Democratic side the delegates are more liberal.

The parties' methods of delegate selection also reflect different philosophies. The Republicans like to leave more to the state organizations. The Democrats have moved in the direction of more national party rules. As I have already indicated, the Democrats have abolished winner-take-all; the Republicans still have it, if the state allows. The Democrats require the delegates to declare their preference or their uncommitted status; the Republicans do not. The Democrats are bound for the first ballot; the Republicans only if state law requires it. The Republicans allow primary crossovers; the Democrats do not allow crossovers anymore, which means that Republicans cannot vote in the Democratic primary.

As to format: Before the opening of the convention, there is a temporary roll of delegates set up by the national Committee. These lists are referred to the Credentials Committee, which holds hearings and makes recommendations. In 1952, we had some great battles at the credentials level in both parties. In the Republican party there was a great fight between Senator Robert Taft of Ohio and General Eisenhower. The regulars tended to favor Taft and as a consequence there were 68 contested delegates from three southern states—Georgia, Texas and Louisiana. The Taft forces were in control of the credentials committee and voted to seat delegates favorable to Taft. But the Eisenhower people took the issue to the convention floor, and by a vote of 607 to 531 the convention repudiated the credentials committee. And everybody knew at the moment that the vote meant Ike was going to be nominated, and he was. The key vote at that convention was at the credentials level.

The 1972 Democratic convention witnessed an unprecedented number of challenges—twenty-three—to the credentials committee. The principal one, however, was on whether the California delegates should be seated on a winner-take-all basis. McGovern had come in first in the primary, but Humphrey had a very large number of votes, so the question went to the credentials committee which voted to take away 151 delegates from McGovern. But by a vote of 1618 to 1238 on the convention floor, McGovern got the whole state of California and that nailed down his nomination. So the credentials is not just a pro forma thing, but can frequently indicate the balance of forces at the convention.

Now let us go on to the platform. The adoption of the party platform is one of the principal functions of a convention. A committee writes it and presents it to the convention for approval. There are floor fights, because the platform goes to the floor, and we have had some tremendous fights on big issues. In 1860 the Democratic party broke in two over the plank on slavery, thus ensuring the election of Abraham Lincoln, the Republican candidate.

In 1924, at that famous long convention in New York City, the problem was a plank involving the Ku Klux Klan. It was the closest vote in convention history on a platform. Five hundred forty-two and seven-twentieths to five hundred forty-three and three-twentieths. That is how closely some of these things can be contested. Another example was the Civil Rights plank in 1948, when the nomination of Harry Truman, who supported that plank, precipitated a walkout by the southerners.

President Wilson once said that the platform is meant to show that the party knows what the nation is thinking about, what it wishes corrected, what it desires to see attained. A platform may be villed with a lot of pious rhetoric, but nevertheless positions are set out and one can make certain generalizations. The Democratic platform tends to be more pro-labor, the Republican more pro-business; the Democrats rely more on governmental intervention at the national level for the resolution of social problems; the Republicans tend to rely more on the private sector.

After the platform fights, if any, are over, the convention turns to its main business—the nomination of a candidate. There is the very dramatic roll-call of the States: Alabama . . . Alaska . . . Arkansas . . . which is still a thrilling moment at any convention. The States respond by nominating, yielding or passing. So, let us say Alabama does not place anyone in nomination, Alabama may yield to Ohio which may then place someone in nomination. In the old days this was followed by endless seconding speeches, demonstrations on the floor that could last for hours and so on. No more, because TV really prohibits that. It is simply too expensive to have hours-long demonstrations. And so both parties have moved to shorten them. They want their candidates on prime time for the real business of the convention. Then there is another roll-call, asking each state how it votes. If no candidate receives a majority then there is a second roll call, a third, a fourth, and on, perhaps up to the record of 103.

After the presidential nominee is finally chosen, all that remains is the nomination of the vice-presidential candidate, historically the choice of the presidential nominee. Adlai Stevenson in 1956 electrified the convention when he let it go to the floor, and Estes Kefauver of Tennessee who had been very successful in the primaries was nominated in a free vote. Historically, the vice-presidency has been used to balance the ticket east with west, north with south, wet with dry, or what have you. For example, in 1928 Al Smith favored the repeal of prohibition. We had to have a vice-president who was on the other side, and so, Joe T. Robinson of Arkansas was chosen.

Now, having looked at the convention system we must ask: who can become president in this country? The constitutional requirements are very simple. Thirty-five years of age. A native-born citizen of the United States. A lot of people can meet those requirements, and yet the number of citizens who can be president is extremely limited. The term "availability" is used to describe the personal, social and political characteristics of those who are in practical and political—rather than constitutional—terms really eligible.

In our present state of political development women could not be nominated, nor could a Black. Neither major party at this time is prepared to do this, although minor parties do nominate persons who do not have the requisite characteristics. For example, Barry Commoner, a distinguished biologist who is Jewish, has an independent party in 1980 and his vice-presidential candidate is an American Indian woman. Now that ticket is doomed to failure and they know that. What Commoner wants to do is to dramatize the importance of certain issues to the future of this country— environmental issues, ecological issues, and so on. He has no expectation whatsoever of becoming President of the United States.

Minor parties are free to nominate whoever they want and in fact sometimes nominate people without the constitutional qualifications. The major party candidates historically have been white, Protestant, males, who are good family men, although we have broken a little into that: John Kennedy was the first Roman Catholic to be elected, and we now consider people who have been divorced—if Ronald Reagan is elected he will be the first divorced person to ever occupy that office. We will try to move next toward the inclusion of women, Blacks, Jews and so on. American Indians really have a long way to go before they could be elected.

There are other characteristics of availability. Most presidential candidates have been from large states. Most have been ex-governors or members of Congress. Occasionally a military hero is nominated. In recent years we have had mostly members of the United States Senate and Vice Presidents.

Now, we can also distinguish various types of nominations. Some of them are wholly consensual, that is the person gets 100 percent on the first ballot, like Roosevelt in 1936. There was no question of course; he got every vote, and it was all over in five minutes.

Similarly with Eisenhower in 1956, when he was renominated; and with Johnson in 1964 and Nixon in 1972. These consensual nominees are leading candidates whose support is so broad that opposing candidates have no chance whatsoever.

The semi-consensual candidate is the provisional nominee who is popular with the rank and file, supported by the leaders, and acknowledged as the likely candidate-to-be. They have survived the primaries, ended the pre-convention period as the front runner, and are much stronger than any alternative, but not dead sure. Stevenson in 1956, Kennedy in 1960, and Nixon in 1968 would be examples.

And then we have the nonconsensual situation, where there are real battles characterized by factional conflict, where the leaders and the rank and file may diverge, or no single candidate emerges and remains the leading contender to the end. Wendell Willkie in 1940 would be illustrative of such a non-consensual nominee. Also Stevenson in 1952 and McGovern in 1972.

Despite all the above, we must make special mention of 1976 because that was an extraordinary election year in both parties. In the Republican party you had Gerald Ford, an incumbent, albeit the first non-elected president in American history, almost denied the nomination even though he enjoyed the support of almost all of the Republican Governors, Senators, Congressmen, State Chairmen, and even such conservatives as former candidate Barry Gold-water. He won the nomination by the closest vote in Republican convention history—1,187 to 1,070 for Ronald Reagan.

In the Democratic party, you have a true outsider coming from almost total obscurity, James Earl Carter III. His very sophisticated managerial team had studied the rules—the McGovern rules—had entered early, and relied very heavily on primary and caucus victories, on direct mail, on the electronic media—on all the new methods of campaigning to mobilize a constituency. Carter's nomination was a striking manifestation of what has been called the "new politics." He demonstrated that a candidate without standing as a national party figure could come through the whole nominating process and win without the support of the leadership. Carter and Reagan in 1976 dramatized what may be the most important fact about contemporary nominating politics in the United States: the inability of either major party to control the nomination for the nation's most important office.

Now what are the prospects? The 1980 Republican convention is clearly going to be a consensual convention; in fact it will be a coronation. It will be over on the first ballot. There is no question, nobody disputes Reagan has the nomination. There will be some platform fights, maybe a little flurry on the floor but nothing much. The Democratic convention will either be semiconsensual or, depending on what the committee forces do, nonconsensual. There is no question but that Carter has the delegates. Carter won 24 primaries. He got almost 10 million votes. Kennedy got just over seven million votes. Carter has 1900 votes out of 3,331. Kennedy has about 1200. Carter has the votes. Yet there are substantial differences in the positions of the two camps that may provide some fireworks on the floor. What is most interesting is the Kennedy position that the delegates should vote their conscience because they are trying to rewrite the rules, which presents some tremendous problems. It is changing the rules in mid-stream, asking the convention to repudiate the McGovern rules and to say that those people who ran committed to Carter in a particular state and won a position as delegates should not be bound by that, which is contrary to the existing rules. And they can be changed. Each convention is a sovereign body and can change those rules. No matter how the issue is resolved in 1980 it is one which will have to be confronted in the future.

Some people think that what has happened particularly in the Democratic party since 1972 or 1976 has been a disaster. But what criteria should we use to evaluate the new nominating process?

How good is the process? How good are the candidates who are selected? Do we select candidates who have a reasonable chance to win the election and to serve the nation successfully as President? Those would be the best criteria.

The parties find themselves in an apathetic even hostile environment. The party system of the 1980's is not the party system of the 1960's much less the 1930's. The fundamental theory of the reformers—that a restructured and more democratically representative party would result in an organization more responsive to contemporary political and social concerns—was in error. It has given extremists, outsiders, and media types much more power. It has taken power from the political leaders who are generally much closer to the system, who have more at stake in the system, and who have more knowledge of the system. There is really no going back to the old days of the kingmakers. We cannot do that. But there should be a greater representation of political leaders in the process.

A distinguished political scientist, Professor Thomas Cronin, has argued that Americans are very contradictory in expectations about Presidential nominees. They want the President to be decent and just, but they also want him to be powerful, and skillful, and decisive and they want him to unite the country, which is a very difficult thing to do except in time of war or under great emergencies. They want him to be above politics, but they also want him to be skillful politically. They want a common man. But a man capable of a very uncommon performance. They want him to be reassuring, but also bold in time of crisis.

Perhaps they want too much; no one can fill all of these various roles. One thing to note is that the presidential selection process brings out qualities and requires qualities quite different from those needed to govern. In other words the best candidate in the primaries, the one who emerges from the nominating process is not necessarily the person who will be the most skillful and most successful president.

The old rules—the old bosses—gave us Franklin Delano Roosevelt. The new rules gave us McGovern and Carter and Reagan.

So we really have the problem of improving the process. We could tinker with the rules here and there, strengthen them, change them. But improving the process as regards who will win the nomination and who will be an effective president is really related to very fundamental things, to the values, the belief structures of the American people at any given time. The issues which they think are of paramount importance.

Modern communications technology; the great demographic changes in the United States; the place of the United States in world politics. These are the things that fundamentally shape the presidency, and reform is more than a matter of changing the rules. The reforms we have instituted have weakened parties, they have aided pressure groups, they have enhanced the power of the press excessively. But no rules can guarantee good nominees and successful presidents. It is an article of faith in the American creed that for every ill there is a remedy. Experience so far with party reform has taught us that for every remedy there may also be an ill.

PATERSON: When we talk about the nominating process I would never separate out any one item from among primaries, caucuses, conventions, federal financing. We must talk about all the rules we have established. They mean absolutely zero when you get to the convention if you have the votes. The response of the Carter people to a question posed by a Kennedy delegate on the rules committee—"Are you telling us that a delegate is mandated to vote for the candidate for whom he pledged support even if that candidate is subsequently convicted of a double act of murder?"—was remarkable. The answer was a forthright, "Yes." Which is no answer. It may have been forthright, but it was not right. The answer is: If the candidate was convicted of a double murder and we disagreed with the murder the delegates should vote for someone else.

Now, as to convention delegates being amateurs. In 1972 there were more persons as delegates who had minimal prior political experience than in the history of all conventions.

But by 1976 it had swung back, and I would bet you that if we go through the 1980 delegates it will have swung back even further.

Why? Candidates, when they have a chance of selecting delegates, want people they can influence. Now, some influence you may consider a little seamy. It may be that I can take your job, if you did not vote the way I wanted, or it could be that the president of a union could make it very hard for a member of his union who did not vote the way the union wanted him to vote.

Al Shanker, President of the United Federation of Teachers in New York City, will meet with the 26 delegates from New York State who are members of his union and express his sentiments before they go into the convention. You may consider that an extreme influence. But we know that what the Carter people sought this time was a consensual nomination, and since they controlled the government, they could do as cabinet members have announced. "If you do not support us Madame Mayor of Chicago, you will not get federal funding." "Mr. Mayor of Gary, Indiana, you will go along with us or you will be embarrassed by the failure of federal funds to bail out your budget deficits." We have cities in this country like Cleveland where they raise revenues only sufficient to pay for the most immediate services: police, fire, sanitation. So that delegates from these places are to a very considerable extent controlled delegates. Their chance of revolting against an incumbent is minimal.

But we never know who can win. The beauty of some candidates has been in that while people thought they could not win, they have stuck to it and gotten support. Jimmy Carter is the best example of this system. We have heard all the reasons given why he got it. He learned the rules. How did he learn the rules? In 1974 two years before he ran for president, the Democratic National Committee appointed Jimmy Carter as chairman of its congressional reelection committee. He travelled the country to support congressional candidates who were Democrats. He installed his own man, Hamilton Jordan, in the Democratic National Committee to honor invitations to wherever he wanted to go. They learned the rules, though some maintain that a "conspiracy" put Carter in power. Carter also got a lot of lucky breaks, if you do not believe the conspiracy theory.

R.W. Apple of the *New York Times,* wrote a front page story on Jimmy Carter's victory in the Iowa caucuses, and that projected him as a major candidate. Now, you could call that luck or an accident, if you do not believe in conspiracy. If you do not believe in vested self-interest, call it something else. But why would Apple be sent out to cover that story? And why was it given the play it received in the *New York Times!*

Now, as to changing the present system. When you talk about reforms, reforms will occur. But only one way in the Democratic party: if President Carter is renominated and is defeated. If he is reelected there will be no changes. Because they would have to be considered by the incumbent president and he controls his party;

that is our system. Changes would be considered a slap in the face of the president. They would be considered a criticism of a system that had produced that presidency. But if Jimmy Carter is defeated you will see many of these reforms occur. You will see the same coalitions that currently feel thwarted coming back together to rewrite some of the reforms. Meanwhile there are some interesting reforms already occurring.

One comes from the fact that in 1972 George McGovern did not give his acceptance speech until 1:00 in the morning. The party leaders vowed that that would never happen again, and they have acted to tighten up the convention. In 1972 you could nominate a candidate for president or vice-president upon filing a petition with 50 authenticated signatures of delegates. That means you could nominate someone with 50 out of 3000 delegates. Ronald Dellum, the Congressman from California, was nominated for vice-president in 1976 and made quite a speech in declining the nomination. In 1972, Julian Bond, then a Georgia State Representative, was nominated; he was too young but he got a chance to make a speech he wanted to make. It is now decreed that to be nominated you need 10 percent of all the delegates. That means more than 300, and the major candidates who control delegates are not going to release their people to sign.

Another reform that will probably go through will deal with the ways and means of assuring candidate accountability to the party platform. Right now the party platform means nothing. It is worth only the paper it is printed on, the time taken to write it. The significance of a party platform is revealed by keeping one thing in mind: you have never heard a single paid advertisement by a political party expounding on the greatness of their platform. Once it is written they want it buried. Why? The candidate does not want to hear about it anymore. Why should he? Maybe there are things he does not want or agree with. He would rather talk about the things that the polls tell him the public wants to hear about.

Finally we ought to say a word about that—what do the people want? And how should political leaders respond to public opinion?

We have so many systems of finding out what people think. We have polled them, we have surveyed them, we do everything. Now, we even have a TV system where people ask questions, press a button, and the answer comes right back instantaneously. Well one of the things the media have done is to conduct what they call post-election surveys. The moment you walk out of the voting booth somebody is there to ask you a question. Who did you vote for and why? There was one overwhelming reaction that came back from our primary elections, from the people, who voted for Carter or against him—they all said, "It really does not matter who the President is because he cannot do anything."

You know what they were saying he could not do anything about? We have an 18 percent prime interest rate and an almost 20 percent inflation rate and a virtual stoppage of new housing construction in this country, and so on through a long list of items. And they were saying they did not think it made any difference who is the president. But it is supposed to make a difference. If it does not then there is something wrong with our governmental structure. If the President—who submits proposals to Congress and who ultimately signs bills that become laws—has no influence on the destiny of this country, then there is something wrong either with the structure or there is something wrong with the people we vote for.

Which is why we need politics and political parties and leaders who are politicians. Franklin Delano Roosevelt was famous for one thing—he was an astute, activist, politician. He may not have projected that image, but we know that is what he was. Abraham Lincoln—the Great Emancipator—got elected because he was a good politician. Six of his opponents ended up in his cabinet. And that was not dirty politics. It got something done.

If you have a President and he cannot get things done, he is useless to this country. And if we have a process that produces such Presidents, then we need a different process.

VI

Presidential Campaigns: Strategies and Tactics

Richard M. Pious
Robert C. Weaver

PIOUS: Let us look at a few factors which form the context for examining election strategy and tactics.

First the American political parties tend to be non-ideological. That does not mean that they do not take positions that can be defined as being on the right or on the left, but that their essence is not to have a definable ideology in the European sense. We also know that American parties are decen¬tralized and federalized, organized from the county to the state level and that the national organizations are quite weak. The Democratic organization is attempting to strengthen itself nationally, but basically we are still dealing with state parties.

Another very important thing is that from the 1970's on our voters have tended to be consumer rather than party oriented, and this I think is a fundamental change. That is to say, in the past you wanted more than anything else to know about a voter's party identification. Are you a Democrat? Are you a Republican? That could probably predict more than ideology, more than stands on issues about how that person would vote in a presidential election. But this is no longer true. Both in the primaries and the general election we have consumer-oriented voters. The candidate and the party are selling a product, and voters now operate and act as consumers.

Another very important point—again as context for looking at the general election strategy and tactics, my particular subject—is the low turnouts. Now we are at a level where 53 or 54 percent of the eligible adults in the electorate actually vote. That is not the same as saying of those registered to vote. If you look at registered voters, we have about sixty-five or seventy percent of the eligibles.

But if you look at eligible adults in the United States who vote we are down to 53 or 54 percent, and it may well go under 50 percent in 1980. It is, for example, an astonishing figure that of eligibles from ages 18 to 34 less than half are registered to vote at the present time. Now it may well be that in the flush of the election excitement we get somewhat over half of that group. It is also true that of all adults eligible to vote in the United States, only two-thirds are registered to vote right now. Again, that may go up a few percentage points as you get voter registration drives. But the context is declining partisanship and lower turnouts.

Another important aspect of the political setting is that our elections are nationalized and are disaggregated. Let us take the jargon term first, disaggregated. What I mean here is that increasingly through the 1960's, 1970's to today the presidential elections (including the primaries in which presidential electors are chosen as well as the general election in November) has become an election standing by itself. There will not be many other elections on most state ballots. Just as in the primary season, it is increasingly the case that the only contest in that primary season is for the presidential delegates.

What has been happening is that more and more of the elections at the state level—for Mayor, Governor, State Legislature, whatever—are being moved out of that four-year presidential cycle. They are being moved into the off-year cycle, that is 1982, 1986, 1990, that cycle of non-presidential even years, or they are being moved into the odd-year cycle. State politicians do this deliberately. Delib¬erately, because the presidential election represents to them the most fundamentally unstable aspect of the American political system. The most erratic. The most unpredictable.

Therefore, disaggregating elections means moving other state and local elections out of the presidential cycle. And this obviously means that the presidential election becomes more and more nationalized. People must vote for the President on the basis of that election alone, and not because of what is happening in state and local parties or in the state and local political context. So that the presidential system, you might say, has cut adrift, cut its moorings away from the state and local contexts. This has been occurring increasingly. You will find, for example, tremendous, volatile shifts in voting behavior at the presidential level which you will not find when you are looking at votes for Congress, votes for State Legislature, votes for local offices. There you have much more stability, much more predictability.

Now let us move to the choices in campaign strategy. Here you have certain elements among which to choose from and among which to give priority. Obviously one is to make a partisan appeal, another is to emphasize your candidate, a third is to emphasize issues, and a fourth is to present to the electorate a clear-cut ideological choice. There are other factors that can be emphasized or de-emphasized, but this would be the broad kind of division.

To begin with, let us look at the failure of ideological campaigns. Taking Goldwater and McGovern as examples there are data that suggest that an ideological appeal not only tends to solidify the opposition around its candidate, but also tends to lead to defection by members of one's own party. Goldwater in 1964 frightened one-fifth of the Republican electorate out of his party; McGovern in 1972 did even worse on his side, frightening or angering people out of the Democratic party. So that to run a campaign that either is ideological or is perceived to be ideological seems to involve great loss. The probability of loss is high, the corresponding advantages, in fact, seem to be low.

This does not necessarily mean that a Reagan might not choose to do this. There might be reasons why he would choose an ideological campaign. But past history suggests that the track record of those who do it is not all that good. The ideological campaigns have always operated on the assumption that you can bring in non-voters, and remember that is now close to 46 percent of the eligibles. For every voter that you have, you have almost one non-voter, a new potential consumer of your product as it were. So the ideological campaigns have assumed that you can woo non-voters and you can get crossovers from the other party into your party. For example, the conservative ideological campaign begins with the premise that more people identify themselves as conservatives or moderates than identify themselves as liberals. This is true especially of large numbers of non-voters. When they are asked, they will say they are conservative. Therefore, the assumption is that there are millions and millions of conservatives who do not register to vote and do not vote because they are turned off by the non-ideological nature of the party system. But if given a real choice, an ideological choice, a conservative choice, they will rush in and will vote.

Now similarly the McGovern campaign on the liberal side had what was known as the 60-60 strategy. What they said was, the young people of this country, the 18-34's, are predominantly liberal; they are with it, with the times, being with the times is to be liberal, and what we will do is we will get 60 percent of these people to register and we will get 60 percent of these people to vote for us.

Now as it happened, in retrospect, you might have called that the 40-40 result. You get around 40 percent of these people registering, and you get about 40 percent of them voting for the liberal. So occasionally there are cases of tremendous miscalculation in the system. But to run an ideological campaign usually assumes that you will break up the opponent's coalition, break up his party through defections, and that you will take advantage of the tremendous numbers of people who do not vote and who one can assume will continue not to vote in 1980.

Next we have campaigns that emphasize the appeal of party. The problem with partisan campaigns tends to be not so much on the Democratic side, but on the Republican side. The Republicans simply do not have that many identifiers. They run 20 to 25 percent of the overall electorate, if you take into account that they vote at higher levels than Democrats, they run maybe 30 percent of the registered voters. And these figures are soft figures, they change from election to election. The Republicans just do not have the bodies there, so to run a completely partisan campaign on the Republican side is essentially to run a losing campaign, to run a badly losing campaign.

However, Republicans do have certain advantages going for them. In most elections in modern times Republicans have won massively in the independent vote. The independent vote, while nominally independent in partisan terms seems very amenable to Republican appeals. In fact one of the few times that Republican candidates have not won this vote was in the Goldwater-Johnson campaign. That is to say, where an ideological appeal was made.

Therefore, the problem for the Republicans is, on the one hand, to maintain their coalition. It may only be 25 percent, but that is the 25 percent they have got. They would be foolish to throw any of that away. And also to reach out and to widen their margin of independent voters and of weak Democratic identifiers. Here we should note that people who call themselves independent Democrats, will finally wind up voting for the Democratic ticket; people who call themselves weak Democrats will very often switch and defect at high rates.

Nobody knows why this is so. The people who conduct surveys are, at present, trying to figure out why, because you would almost assume it would be the other way—to call yourself an independent Democrat should mean a high rate of defection, higher than a weak Democrat—but it seems to work the other way. All of the computer people are trying to go back and figure out whether it is the wording of their questions or some underlying variable and some day they will discover what this all means.

Anyway, the Republicans, as a strategy, want to maintain their base, but then they want to reach out to independents and to weak Democrats. And the way to do that especially, is to go after the young. You go after the young, even though they have very low voting rates, because they have a very high predisposition to consider themselves independents, or to consider themselves very weak party identifiers. So the Republicans should be going after the youth. It does not necessarily mean they always do, but they should be doing that and they should be consolidating their position.

For the Democrats, as the majority party, to run a completely partisan campaign is one very acceptable strategy for them stemming really from Roosevelt and the New Deal coalition. They can win and they can win big with a highly partisan campaign such as the campaign in 1936.

On the other hand, they can also win and win just as big with a Lyndon Johnson consensus campaign. Johnson went out in 1964 and he would say to people, "Come on down to the speakin' tonight. There's gonna be the speakin' tonight." It was this sort of cornpone southern style that he used, and people would come on down to the speakin'. And then he would tell them all the things that he had done for them in the Great Society, and all the things that the Great Society was going to do in the near future. And he would conclude with a phrase that would go something like this. He would say, "You know, we Democrats are for a mighty lot of things, and we are against a might few." It meant, "We are the party of positivism and what you want is what we want, and what we want is what you want. We are an inclusive party. We will include you in our grand coalition, whether you be a Democrat or a Republican." The great consensus. Democrats can win big both ways. Republicans can only win big, or win at all, one way. They cannot win running a completely partisan campaign.

Running on the issues involves certain media techniques, and gets us into the field of media politics. If you run a media campaign on a non-ideological, consumer-oriented basis, you will characterize the opposition as being irresponsible or incompetent. You will thematize, that is, present some theme of your own rather than a very reasoned discussion of the issues. You will present a very short theme, usually in the form of a slogan which has an emotive, emotional effect, much more than a cognitive or intellectual effect. You will visualize, that is, present visuals that enable people to see themselves and the party in a very positive light. And, of course, you will simplify. And what you will produce essentially is what we call the "happy commercial."

The happy commercial—I do not know whether or not this is an American invention, but I suppose we might as well claim credit for it—is the Pepsi-Cola commercial or the Coca-Cola commercial or the airline commercial; a catchy theme song, a catchy tune. We had this in 1976, when the Ford campaign rested its visuals on what was essentially a Coca-Cola commercial. It showed happy people, it showed America on the move, and it had a theme song which went something like, "I'm feeling good about America; America is feeling good about me . . ." or something like that. We know that around the world when a politician uses this kind of technique it is known as the Americanization of the campaign.

Well one can do this and one can use new politics techniques and get very far with it. In fact, this is primarily how the Republicans have managed to overcome their minority party status. What tends to happen is the Republican nominee cuts himself loose from his own party, relying on the party organizations to deliver whatever votes they are going to deliver and relying on Republican identifiers to deliver whatever votes they will deliver, and then tries to get the broad mass of weak identifiers from both parties and independent voters and the youth by running a strong media campaign, a very simplified media campaign.

Now generally if you look at traditional party competition, the standard approach was to use what is referred to today as "spatial competition." Spatial competition means taking the major central issue—which in the American system is usually an economic issue, or what is called a "more or less" issue (more for one group, less for another; for example, more regulation or less regulation, more deficits or less deficits, etc.)—and bundle these up into a set of issues, place them on a continuum, and have one party be farther to the right, the other party farther to the left. In our two-party system the logic of spatial competition is to move both parties towards the center. There is an ultimate logic that says they both should wind up right in the center. Parties never get there because of the internal dynamics of their own coalitions and their history and a variety of other factors, but the logic is to move towards the center.

Increasingly in the 1970s and 1980s, this sort of appeal does not make all that much sense, because many issues are no longer spatial, more or less issues. Instead they are what are referred to as "valance" issues. Valance issues are "yes or no" issues. Abortion—yes or no. Gun control—yes or no.

Sanctity of the family—yes or no. Busing—yes or no. A whole series of foreign policy issues which are increasingly expressed by the electorate as for it or against it, not partly for it or partly against it.

What can happen in a media politics campaign is that you can immediately go for the valence issue and put your candidate on one side of it or the other. And you can do so without necessarily providing any real coherence. I believe that our campaign rhetoric, our campaign appeals are not only becoming simpler than in the past, but they are also displaying less coherence than ever before. Some people are arguing that we have a more polarized and ideological campaigning system, moving toward a conservative party and a liberal party, but I do not see it that way at all. I see these valence issues as being identified by pollsters, and then candidates using media politics appeals to go right for those issues and not worrying too much about the coherence of it.

Presentation of presidential candidates is another campaign factor. The candidates can be presented in a number of ways. As my colleague at Columbia, Henry Graff has said, "The dirty secret of American politics is that we love a war hero." We are not the only country that loves a war hero of course, but this is our politics and unfortunately we do not have war heroes available at the present time. You have to win wars to have war heroes and we have not done that recently.

So we have the present unavailability of war heroes. On the other hand—possibly this is a low blow—one can substitute someone who has played the part of a war hero in the cinema, but that is a separate story. Instead I would say most candidates are today playing the role of Mr. Outsider. They are de-emphasizing their Washington experience. In fact, to run for president these days it helps not to hold public office. That just slows you down, because you have to be in Washington or the State House. It is probably much better not to have a job anymore, and to play Mr. Outsider. That is the way Carter capitalized on discontent in 1976, and Reagan certainly will do this in 1980. Anderson seems to be trying to have it both ways, with the appeal of competence on the one hand, but being outside the party system on the other.

The incumbent strategy always seems to be to act presidential. To act presidential has meant to stay in the Rose Garden. We had this in '72 with Nixon, in '76 with Ford, in 1980 with Carter. A lot of this, incidentally really started in 1964. Many people still assume that Lyndon Johnson went around the country triumphantly campaigning. That really was not the way it happened. Johnson spent most of the time in the White House acting presidential. He made a trip up to New England to do a minimal amount of campaigning and the trip was wildly successful. The people just wanted to come out and see Lyndon Johnson, and he established a rapport with the crowd and everybody came back somewhat stunned at how well things had gone. Then they began scheduling a great many more trips. It was actually a scheduling adjustment in the Johnson campaign. And then he did quite a bit of campaigning.

But the strategy for a president is presumably, stay in the White House, act presidential and hopefully do something that is presidential. Take some major action, orchestrate some major action.

Anderson in the 1980's presents the beginning of what might be a realignment of the parties, because a third candidate very often is a waystation. People vote for a third candidate on the way toward a fundamental switch of party allegiance. Anderson could be that, or alternatively, Anderson could mark the beginning of the real decomposition of the American political parties. Eliminate the middleman. Move right to a choice between a notable with high public exposure and the electoral college choice. After all, the way our constitutional selection system operates, we do not need nominations, we do not need primaries. We do not need any of that. We simply need electors meeting in their separate states providing a majority in the electoral college.

Anderson can go around the entire process in which he is an outsider and has been defeated and move directly to the final choice. His poll support is likely to be highly volatile for reasons that I will get to shortly. I do not believe that Anderson will ultimately remain at 21 percent or so. His strategy has to be to convince many more people to vote for him and to move up much higher, not only in the general polls but also on a state by state basis because we have a state by state, winner-take-all system.

Assuming that he gets on the ballot in most states, which by now I think is a reasonable assumption, his strategy is to raise between $10 and $15 million dollars, and to spend all of that money—all of it—on media campaigning especially dealing with valance issues. Anderson does not have a party; he is not forming a party. Every dollar raised other than overhead costs, can go immediately into mass media political campaigns. Themes, simplification, visualization, drama, hitting the valence issues.

Ultimately Anderson is hoping for a three-candidate lottery. A soon as you create a three-candidate situation, it can be expressed in game theory as a lottery with three possible winners. Number one is your preference. For many people that preference might be

Anderson. Number three is the worst outcome, that which they fear the most. For certain people that might be Carter; for other people that might be Reagan. Number two, the second choice, is simply the one in the middle about whom people say, "I am not enthusiastic about that person, but I am not having nightmares about him either." And the hope is that they eventually say, "I am so afraid of getting three if I vote for one, I had better vote for two."

Thus Anderson's strategic problem is to convince people that by voting for him the worst they will get in their state is number two. It is expressed as a lottery because eventually you can use mathematical notation. What you can say to people is, what odds do I have to give you between one and three, to induce you to actually vote for one? If there is a 90 percent chance that Anderson will win the state, will you vote for Anderson? Suppose you say it is 50-50, that you get Anderson. You might get Anderson, but on the other hand, you might get the worst outcome. Would you still try for Anderson? Now you are going to start to get defection. And these again can be plotted mathematically. At a certain point when the probability declines, all of a sudden people will defect from Anderson. They will say, "I like Anderson, but I am so afraid of choice number three, that I had better vote for choice number two." Obviously this is what the other two candidates are banking on. That they can keep Anderson at a level at which the lottery does not provide sufficient odds state by state to vote for him.

Paradoxically, the Anderson strategy would be much better off not attacking Reagan as a horrible candidate who will start World War III, because if you do that it will drive an awful lot of people away from the lottery and into the number two choice. I think what Anderson should say is, "You can live with all three of us. Why not try me? If you don't get me and you get number three, you'll still be alive. The country won't go up in flames."

The Reagan choice it seems to me is either to follow the logic of his delegates and his inner circle and possibly his own instincts and move towards a conservative appeal and try to go for that hidden group out there who are just waiting for a conservative candidate. Or he could run a non-ideological, media and independent-oriented campaign. He has several alternatives. He could be a regional candidate, the candidate of the Sun Belt, which is a heck of a large region, really constituting more than half the country at this point. Or he could move towards a completely national campaign, which I think he will do. Finally he could either emphasize the distributional and coalitional issues which are primarily the spatial competition and say that he is the candidate of the-right-of center on economic issues or he could move very heavily into the valence issues. I think in part he will try to do both, and that may in fact weaken him. He can attack the opposition or he can emphasize the positive. The more he attacks, the more strident a tone he takes, the more probably he will be playing into Carter's hands. He will come on hot in what McCluhan calls a "cool medium."

Carter's big problem is to keep Anderson from becoming viable. They have failed already in attempts to keep Anderson off the state ballots, and they have gotten a great deal of negative publicity. It has reinforced the fundamental basis of Anderson's strength, which is the good government types and the procedural types. They are strengthened by the thought that their candidate has staved off a low blow from the Carter camp.

Carter will have to regain the Kennedyites, who thus far have shown no inclination to bend at all or to be accommodating. His next problem is how to win support in the Northeast and the South, two regions that very often have antithetical interests dating all the way back to the beginning of our nation. Does he act presidential and defend his record? Possibly not. Does he attack the opposition? That puts him down at the same level as Reagan in a certain sense. He has one alternative which I do not think he will adopt, although it is an honorable tradition in local and state politics: to repudiate and run against his own record.

In the City of New York we have had two mayors who did that. Mayor John Lindsay and Mayor Robert Wagner, both of whom ran against their own record. In both cases they ran against the original party organizations that nominated them and both won.

I do not think Carter is going to do this, but it is an interesting ploy. If nothing else works and he is way behind in the election, who knows what he might try to pull.

WEAVER: I would like to open this by sort of saying what I am not. I am not a political scientist, I am not a politician. In fact in some quarters I am supposed to be a very lousy one. I am a quasi-bureaucrat who tried to seduce a bureaucracy. I think I am a public administrator. And I am still a liberal who does not apologize for being so. I had anticipated that I was going to find myself largely in agreement with the previous speaker, so I had gotten a retreat position in case I were. That is to say, some remarks which I think will be supportive and probably add something to what he has said.

I must say that I do agree with him particularly in his very brilliant presentation of Anderson's role and strategy. I can think of only one thing I would add. I think this strategy makes a great deal of sense primarily because so many Democrats are turned off as far as the present incumbent is concerned, which makes the strategy implicit in what he said a great deal more viable than it might otherwise be.

Let me start by outlining the milieu in which the 1980 campaign is occurring, a milieu which has raised serious questions among academics, commentators, editors, and voters as to Americas' capacity to govern itself.

There are many elements involved. They include the concerted attack upon the Great Society articulated by the neo-conservatives, many of whom are former liberals and socialists with great prestige among intellectuals and impressive literary talents. This movement has given credence to the notion that governmental action to deal with public issues is largely futile and reliance should almost exclusively be on the operation of the market.

And then there are the breakdowns in the power of political organizations and the erosion of party discipline in the Congress with the consequent rejection by Congress of Presidential leadership; the increasing emergence of the Executive Office of the President as the center of policy formation and an indispensable instrument for Congressional relations; and the influence of the media on public affairs and the popularization of the presidential nomination.

While there is, in my opinion, an exaggeration of the impact of these and other recent structural changes, such as the growing importance of presidential primaries, changes in the organization and functions of Congress, and the impact of the radio and TV upon the political process, nonetheless these changes are significant. As far as the presidential nomination and elections are concerned, developments in the media mean greater exposure of the candidates and greater clamor for accountability on the part of the incumbent.

They also mean that the candidates are de facto selected before the platforms upon which they are supposed to run have been formulated. To a degree never approached before, the personality of the candidate becomes crucial in the selection process. And candidates are to a large extent packaged and sold largely on TV.

Let me reiterate. This is a matter of degree. Much that seems new is not. Generals have always been attractive presidential candidates, witness Washington, Grant and Eisenhower. Flamboyant personalities have always had great appeal. As a child I was impressed by accounts of Theodore Roosevelt as an independent "Bull Moose" candidate.

Later Woodrow Wilson was known as a scholar and Charles Evans Hughes looked like a president. The images of candidates were created and became influential before radio or TV. After 1932, however, when radio brought Franklin D. Roosevelt into the American home, the matter of image-making has become more important, and TV has added another dimension.

TV and the primaries were largely responsible for John F. Kennedy's nomination; the 1960 TV debates, presenting an articulate, clean-cut and attractive Kennedy versus a less impressive and devious-looking Nixon, had much to do with the latter's defeat.

What has occurred is that judgments of presidential candidates' personalities has become, to a large degree, an evaluation based upon what social scientists call "primary data." The voter can see and listen to the evidence for himself rather than, as in the past, be dependent upon secondary sources. The latter of course are still available in the form of radio and TV commentaries, as well as news stories, periodical articles, and editorials. All of this has changed the nature of presidential elections. Harry Truman's definition of the party platform as a contract between the party and the people was an exaggeration when pronounced, and it is basically inaccurate today. For increasingly we look more to the man than to the party or its platform. In part this is a sophisticated approach, since Presidents have not been loathe to repudiate platforms; in part it is a reflection of the erosion of political parties mentioned above, and in part it flows from the growing importance of primaries and media exposure.

Thus we now have the situation where the Republican platform is basically a conservative document, which a-mong other things repudiates the Equal Rights Amendment for women, supports a Constitutional amendment to protect the lives of unborn children, places almost exclusive dependence upon the market to solve economic problems—even those of blacks, many of which actually result from past operation of the market—advocates increasing defense expenditures, and champions state's rights.

One New York Times columnist writes:

> For many Americans and many politicians who would lead them there is a desire for remembered values of the past. It is another key to the Carter and Reagan successes so far in 1980. Not only do they argue, for example, for reduced government spending, but they also convey stability in their own lives. This is an important element in measuring the kind of conservatism that is winning in 1980. No matter how hard polltakers try to get people to focus on ideology in their answers, many of those who call themselves conservative plainly are referring to their lifestyles, not their views on welfare reform, aid to the cities and other issues. The flexibility in the proposed Republican platform underscores a central truth about American politics. At one time or another, it may be alright to be liberal or conservative, but it is better to seem pragmatic and it always hurts, as in the case of McGovern, to seem to be extreme or even ideological. The recognition of this is a Carter strength. It has also been a Reagan strength, although many Republicans say they fear that the combination of a conservative platform with a vice presidential choice and an acceptance speech that are perceived to be conservative would make the party seem extreme.

Although the principles of the Democrats and the Republicans as set forth in their parties' platforms will differ, many voters are not paying too much attention to platform. Those that are influenced by them per se seem to be motivated in a negative sense. Thus special interest groups are prone to be alienated by repudiation of their special interests, for example feminists by the rejection of the ERA in the Republican platform.

This is true in part because the issues of the 1980's are recognized as crucial, but the need for effective leadership in the White House is stressed even more. One hears registered voters express dissatisfaction with Carter, Reagan and Kennedy, while many who admire Anderson doubt that he is a viable choice. And at a time when there is great apprehension about America's capacity to govern, about the economy and about foreign affairs, the incumbent is extremely vulnerable.

Those who have no great commitment to any candidate may then tend either to seek a new president or not to go to the polls. Those who are disillusioned about Carter's performance, and there are many of them, may well respond favorably to the extensive TV advertisements which say it is about time to give the Republicans a chance to run the government. Reagan is by far the more polished TV performer. Yet he has developed a weakness, a tendency to "shoot from the lip" when confronted with a question or issue not covered by his text. At times he appears ignorant of the subject or misinformed concerning it. Should Carter be able to exploit this vulnerability he may be able to offset, in varying degrees, the greater financial resources, the apparent unity and the current high expectations of the Republican Party.

As in 1960 TV debates could be a deciding factor. While the Republicans seem to be on the upswing as of now, especially because of the dissatisfaction of the vital middle class and the apprehensions and disillusionments of many blue collar workers and minorities, it would be a mistake to discount the political ability and agility of Jimmy Carter or the propensity for the Republicans to alienate large blocks of voters by an insensitivity to their aspirations and needs.

One thing is clear. The number of blacks who are going to vote for Mr. Reagan or the Republican party is minuscule. The whole economic philosophy of the neo-conservatives and of conservatism, the whole idea of depending upon the market and letting these forces work themselves out is anathema to blacks, who recognize two things:

First that there has to be public intervention in social issues, and secondly that their rights are best protected by a strong Federal Government and not a state's rights party. Here the issues are important. Added to that is the fact that while Jimmy Carter is a little bit in the dog house because he has not produced what he promised to produce, he also has a "good ole' boy" southern approach and he gets along extremely well with blacks as an individual. He knows them, he has lived with them, he has got very strong support among many of them. And my guess is that a large black vote is going to be for Carter, or the black vote will be largely for Carter, among those who vote, with a lot of blacks going fishing. The only real challenge that Carter faces among those who vote among blacks is the Anderson candidacy. And here again I think blacks have a second, third, fourth sense of survival, and they are going to be very much worried about throwing their votes away.

But Carter could nonetheless be in trouble, because there would seem to be some groups—and I think blacks are among them, Jews are among them—who seem to be disaffected with the present administration to a greater degree than might normally be expected. I would include there blue-collar labor as a whole.

You do not need much of a shift to change the election. For example, blacks voted 95 percent for Carter. Well, what if you got a 10 or 15 percent defection? Jews were next in line; Jews voted 85 percent for Carter. What if you got a defection of a quarter of that vote? Blue collar workers, likewise. It seems to me that that kind of shifting, for whatever reasons, does not have to be massive in order to defeat the incumbent. And then of course the next question would be, throw the Anderson candidacy into the thing and what does that do?

VII

Presidential Campaigns: Press, Polls, Packaging

Douglas Ireland
Murray Edelman

IRELAND: America is known for its freedom of the press, but A.J. Liebling, the great critic of the New Yorker magazine, once said that the only way to have freedom of the press is to own one. This is particularly true in America in the period since World War II. We have in the United States today virtually a monopoly press. Of the 7500 weekly newspapers and 1700 daily papers, two-thirds are owned by corporate chains. In only 56 cities in the United States are there competing newspapers of different ownerships.

In most American towns and cities there is one newspaper and one ownership. In too many instances, the newspaper is also owned by the local television station, or the local radio station. So that we have a situation in which access is controlled by a very, very small group of corporate and increasingly multi-national corporations. The top four chains in the United States own 21%—almost one quarter—of the newspapers in the country.
Now, in an electronic age, when television is so terribly, terribly important in shaping the way that the vast majority of the public, of the electorate, of the citizenry, think about political questions, this monopolistic situation is critical.
It is important to go back to the period immediately after World War II and look just for a moment at the political history of this country over the last thirty years, and what it has meant in terms of declaring certain points of view legitimate and certain points of view illegitimate, and therefore accessible or inaccessible to the mass of the citizenry. It is terribly important, and I do not think one can have a real understanding of the nature of American politics and the relationship of the press to politics without understanding the effects of the cold war and the Joe McCarthy period and the witch hunts and the blacklistings that destroyed hundreds of thousands of lives and destroyed the left in this country; unless one understands the terribly chilling impact that thirty years of the cold war have

had on views that are substantially at disagreement with the center right views which dominate American politics.

Let's take the *New York Times,* that great liberal newspaper which is always held out to be the prime example of American journalism at its best. What was the role of the *New York Times* in the cold war period and under Joe McCarthy? Its role was like that of the big moguls in Hollywood—to fire writers and reporters and editors and printers and pressmen who were accused of being Communists. It caused many of them to testify in front of McCarthy's Congressional Committee. This is the attitude that the most "liberal" newspaper in the country took during the witch hunt, during the suppression of free speech in this country. We have never recovered from this. The left has never recovered from this assassination during the cold war at its height, and the press has certainly never recovered its sensibility either. It has never recovered its freedom. Its freedom has been eroded.

Sadly, this is really a reversal of what for many, many years was a terribly vigorous tradition of independent journalism in this country. We used to have a large labor press in the country. People forget that. We used to have news—wire services, news gathering organizations that were supported by the trade unions in the period when the trade unions were political, before they had become enmeshed and co-opted by the corporate system, and before they had their own left wings destroyed by the cold war.

That's all gone, and so now what you have is television, the great eye, the great arbiter of what is legitimate debate and what is not in this country. And television defines the debate from the center to the right. Even on public television, it is terribly difficult for views from the left that are even mildly critical of the Carter Administration, for example, to get a hearing. On the networks, criticism is virtually non-existent.

The points of view considered legitimate in America are increasingly moving to the right. The spectrum for dissent is narrowing, as we see reflected in the American political situation today. One feeds the other. And now we are faced with the prospect—I think the certainty—of Ronald Reagan. This is in no small measure due to television. Gore Vidal once wrote that Reagan will be a success because he is the ultimate star of the late show, equally ubiquitous, equally mythic. In addition, Reagan has managed to master the use of television as a television actor and performer and commentator, to a much greater degree than Mr. Carter has.

The Anderson phenomenon is not simply the expression of disenchantment with the two party system in the period after the scandals of Watergate and Abscam (the FBI plot to entrap and bribe Congressmen, which succeeded so easily). Anderson's success is traceable directly to his ability to use television, to project himself on television.

Politics today in this country has become a capital intensive business. If you do not have a lot of money, you are not going to be successful because you have to have access to radio, to television, to direct mail and other expensive forms of mass communication. Party organizations are really quite irrelevant. The old precinct system, the old commit-teeman system, the ward system, the bosses, the clubs—even the footsoldiers of 1968 and the McCarthy and Robert Kennedy anti-war campaigns—are all irrelevant today. They all pale into insignificance beside the awesome power of radio and television. A costly power—power therefore defined by its very expensive nature as inaccessible to views that are not heavily funded, usually by corporate and special interests.

This is the nexus of issues which I think important to look at as we try to understand the relationship between the press and politics that exists in a country like America, which has so many centers of power, in which power is diffused. It is a symbiotic relationship; one is feeding the other. The elimination of dissent in the cold war period created this terrible, chilling, narrow-minded climate in the press. The press became increasingly more conservative. This fed the conservative mood in the country. Certain views were denied legitimacy. The country moved further to the right, the press responded, and the cycle keeps moving. George Washington University just a couple of weeks ago issued a survey of the three television networks and the way in which they cover politics. It showed that network television has been covering the Republicans significantly more than the Democrats, and that is one reason we can look forward to a very interesting four years under the candidate of television and the candidate of the corporations, Mr. Ronald Reagan.

The George Washington University survey described the contents of the evening news. It usually starts off with about ten minutes of what has happened to the big people, the candidates, because of a philosophy in the media that the office holders make the news. The president makes the news. The president having a cold or a little sniffle is a lot more significant than some kind of labor union winning some kind of contract or some kind of movement agitating someplace.

Then the next ten minutes is often stuff like the latest hurricane or tornado, visually interesting, and usually from the Midwest. Finally it ends up with a few minutes about kooks in California, because that is a cute little ending.

But there are real factors in television. One is you want to keep people interested, and they can just handle so much. One of the problems we have with our surveys is that you can just present so much on the air. In fact, one of the reasons why we have a joint CBS-New York Times poll is that we found that we would collect all this information in our surveys, but we would only put out very little of it, because there was just so much people could handle while watching TV. So what happens is that we put out the big stories on CBS the night before the whole survey is released, and then the Times does a much more thorough analysis the next morning; that is the way the arrangement has worked out.

A lot of people are mystified by polls. Why, they wonder do the various polls often differ in their results. Well, Walter Cronkite was real upset because we wanted him to make this statement after giving our results: "These results have an error of plus or minus 3%." He could not understand why we wanted him to say there was an error on the numbers. But there was one point at which the polls differed by 5 to 10 points—Roper, Gallup, us—we all had different numbers, and then Cronkite started understanding why there is a difference, and now he is happy to make the margin-of-error statement.

We do two main kinds of polls. One is called a national poll, and the other is an election day survey, which is a poll we do as people leave their voting places. In our national poll, we sample 1500 people nation-wide. We talk to them by telephone.

There are two main ways to poll. One you do by telephone, and the other you do by households. People like Gallup and Harris and Roper do households mainly and occasionally telephones. We do exclusively telephones for various reasons. One is that telephone surveys are a lot cheaper, and another is that political surveys can be done well by telephone, unlike consumer stuff where you may want to show pictures and go into much more depth on things. The main problem with telephones is that not everybody has one. About 98% do, though. A few years ago there were not that many telephone surveys, but now more and more people are getting telephones.

I think telephones are probably the best way. When you do it in person, it is a much more costly procedure, and you have to send people into neighborhoods that are dangerous and things like that.

We design our samples so that every phone number in the country has a chance of being selected, and every phone number has the same chance of being selected. One way of doing it is just to pick phone numbers at random. But that is a really costly procedure because if you pick every number at random, what you would find is, that of all possible numbers maybe only 10% are really working numbers. If you just pick numbers at random based on the exchanges, you would find only about 30% working numbers. We have a procedure that gets us about 60% and our technique is a contribution we have made to the whole science of polling.

Now there are a number of reasons why you would get a disparity when you look at the numbers. One of them is just sampling error. There is always some variability in a survey. If you get a large enough sample, you have less variability. So we might show Reagan has 45%, someone else might show Reagan has 47%. That would all be well within the margin of error, and it would be easily explained. But it is a really important concept to keep in mind, because when you read numbers—and a lot of the press does this—they will show Carter 45, Kennedy 43, and the headline will be "Carter leads Kennedy." They might say by a slim margin.

The reality is no one is leading. You do not have enough evidence; you do not know who is winning. Period. We never say someone is leading. We have an understanding with the *Times* and with CBS that we say they are even when that is the case. We do not give our numbers, we just say that they are even. We never try to show a difference unless there really is clearly a difference.

Another source of error is the wording of the question. One of the surveys that Louis Harris has been doing says, "Suppose John Anderson had a good chance of winning. Would you vote for Reagan, Carter or Anderson?" We would just ask "Who would you vote for?" Now he is finding a lot more people want Anderson, but there is a bias in his question because the minute you indicate that someone has a chance of winning you get a little bit of a bandwagon effect from people. So the question wording is real important. You can get vast changes by just how you word a question.

Another factor is where you put your question in the questionnaire. For example, today when we have high unemployment if I started off a questionnaire with questions about the economy—How is the economy doing? Do you have a job? Are you happy with your style of living?—and then I say do you approve of Carter as president, I am going to get a much lower approval rating than somebody who starts off the questionnaire by just saying do you approve of Carter as president. So our first question is always "Do you approve of the president?" Otherwise you cannot compare it from month to month, because you have different substance in the questionnaire.

One of the techniques that Pat Caddell, Carter's pollster, has used is to start off by asking what people think of Carter and of Kennedy. Then he would ask questions about the economy and really raised negative feelings. And then he asked again who you approved, Carter or Kennedy. What he found for most of the campaign was substantial drops in Carter support, which has led a lot of pollsters to say that Kennedy support was hard and Carter support was soft, that Carter support can be moved.

Approval rating can be very important on occasion. For example, it was real useful during Nixon's time, because we were tracking how it was falling and falling, and it started getting to a level where there was no confidence in the president, and that was one of the things that put pressure on him. So polling is one way that the public is heard.

Another kind of poll that CBS does is the election day poll that we do in conjunction with our coverage of the elections. In November, we are going to take a sample of precincts in every state in the country. We have reporters at every precinct. We select the precincts using a random probability method, and as the polls close the reporters phone in the results. We use a very sophisticated method of estimating from these results, and then we look at the error margin on the results coming in, and then we say who is going to win. I am always amazed at this point, because we have made only one mistake in ten years. We have called about 600 races, and we have made one mistake. Every time we call 100 races on election night I feel, "Oh God, this thing works; the polling works, the survey works."

We also station interviewers in each precinct, and they take a sub-sample of the voters as they are leaving the precinct and interview them. Actually we give them a ballot which asks who they voted for and tons of other questions—what issues were important to them, why they voted, things like that.

Using this technique we were able to show that people voted for Kennedy because he had leadership qualities, they voted for Carter because he had honesty and integrity; that people generally agreed with Kennedy more on the issues, but still voted for Carter; that the issue of honesty and integrity—of Chappaquiddick—was really stopping people from voting for Kennedy.

We also found in the Ohio, California, and New Jersey primaries that 20% of the people who said they had supported Carter were considering defection to someone else, and that two thirds of the Kennedy supporters were going to vote for Anderson; that basically things did not look very good for Carter, even though he had just clinched the nomination.

One last point to keep in mind about polls is that they do not predict the future. There was this poll in New York that Lou Harris did where he said Carter was going to win by 7 points and Kennedy ended up winning by 20 points. He is still trying to explain that. He is saying there is this trend that happened two months ago, and he caught it at one point and then a week later it changed. We generally try not to predict who is going to win. We avoid predicting any primary results for that reason, because primaries are amazingly volatile. On the other hand, when you start saying Reagan has 45%, Carter has 28%, Anderson has 20%, it is hard not to see that as some kind of prediction. But the thing to keep in mind is that it is only an accurate statement at the time. Polls are really just a measure of what people think at specific points in time.

VIII

Is This Any Way to Elect a President?

Eugene J. McCarthy
Shirley Chisholm
James Q. Wilson
Steven Brams

McCARTHY: Anyone who has been beaten twice in a presidential election has to believe there is something wrong with the system. And I have been persuaded of that at least twice—once in 1968 running within the Democratic party and once as an Independent in 1976. I would suggest based on these two experiences that there are three things that should be changed in our system.

One is the freedom of the parties to make up their own rules. It is rather arbitrary. They are almost outside the law in making up party rules. And when you get to a convention, why you are in another country. The Democratic party, after the 1980 convention, will have operated with three different sets of rules at three successive conventions, and each time the rules will have determined who got nominated.

In 1968 we operated under the old rules of the party which were sort of traditional. Each state did about what it wanted to do. There were accommodations, since nobody would arbitrarily impose rules if the prospect was that they would cause great division within the party. The old rules, in effect from at least 1948 and more or less determined by each state, operated through 1968. We protested 22 delegations in Chicago in '68 as being unrepresentative and improperly chosen and whatever else we could think of. But the Rules Committee ruled against us on all of them.

Meanwhile in law suits brought in two states the judges had said that if by 1972 these rules were not changed they would enjoin the delegations from the particular states from going to the Convention. So the party as part of their defense of the abuse, passed a resolution in 1968 saying they would change the rules and they did proceed to set up a commission to change the rules with Senator McGovern in charge.

The rules were changed to a degree in 1972 to outlaw what was known as the "unit rule" in non-primary states. But it did not outlaw the "winner-take-all" primaries. Senator McGovern ran under those rules and he won the nomination. He'd helped to write the rules and they were just right for him. He could not have been nominated with the '68 rules. He could not have been nominated with the '76 rules. But the '72 rules were just right for him, because he got his share of the delegates from the non-primary states, and since in the primaries they honored winner-take-all state laws, he got all of California for example. So he could take all of the delegates from a primary state, and also get his share from a non-primary state. Putting the two together, he had a majority.

After that it was obvious that this was unfair because if you are going to allocate non-primary state delegate votes, you should also allocate primary state delegate votes. So they had a new Commission to change the rules. Jimmy Carter was on it, and Jimmy Carter changed the rules, and the 1976 rules were just right for him. Carter could not have been nominated with the '68 rules I do not think, and I am quite certain he could not have been nominated with the '72 rules. But the '76 rules were just right for him because the unit rule did not mean anything in his case since he was going to get the Solid South anyway with or without a primary.

He could afford to give other candidates their share in the non-primary states because that did not amount to anything. But in the primary states, some of those in which it used to go winner-take-all, the party had changed the rules, so if Carter got 30 percent in a primary, he got his share of the delegates. And that did it for him.

In anticipation of 1980 the Carter people did not think they should run again with the '76 rules. So they fixed the rules to make it even more certain that he would get renominated. And since they did it in the name of reform they got liberal support because liberal Democrats will vote for anything called reform. What Carter did was to put in a "threshhold" requirement, which said that if you get below a certain percentage of votes, your votes get thrown into a common pot and are then distributed among those who got more than the threshold—which meant that it was almost impossible to defeat an incumbent president.

These problems arise every twenty or thirty years. I am persuaded now, especially since the two parties have been "legalized" by the

Federal Election Act, that the country itself, the body politic, cannot allow the parties to make up rules as they go along. The only way we can get to this problem may be through Supreme Court decisions in which the principle of one person-one vote is fed back into the party process as it now is in the electoral process.

So I would say rule-making is the first area that should be attacked, because parties act most arbitrarily in regard to it. The second is the Federal Election Law itself. We have had various kinds of election control laws in the states. They have accumulated over the years, in most cases drafted by either Republicans or Democrats to protect themselves against something that happened to them that they did not like.

Most of these laws have gone unchallenged. In 1948 George Wallace challenged some successfully; in 1968 I challenged some successfully; and in 1980 John Anderson challenged some. But it does not last. You challenge, you win a court case, you go away and you come back, and the state legislature has done something worse. So you go to court again and you may win again, but by that time the election may be over or you have spent half your time in court trying to get on the ballot.

In 1976 in New York I was taken off the ballot on the Friday before election by a New York court. We had won our case before the State Board of Elections, which said my independent petition signatures were valid. The Democrats then appealed to a lower court, to a single judge who happened to be a Democrat. He ruled that my signatures were not valid. We then appealed to an intermediate court which had a majority of Republicans. They wanted me on the ballot. They held that my signatures were valid and put me back on. Democrats then appealed to the highest court in New York, which had a majority of Democrats who did not want me on the ballot, and I was taken off the Friday before election.

That was an example of operating under state law. Now along with that we have the Federal Election Law which has been in effect only since 1976, and I do not know what one does about it. Unless the Supreme Court acts, I do not think the Congress will act until it is clear that it is utterly ridiculous. But the effect of the federal law is that the two major political parties in this country have been "legalized". It was done because, on the one hand, the Republicans were so desperate after Watergate that they thought they were going to disappear. So one way to keep themselves alive was to make them legal. So they legalized themselves even at a disadvantage. It was a way of survival and a defense against Watergate.

On the other hand, the Democrats, who controlled the Congress while the law was being passed have much more difficulty raising money, and they figured that they could make themselves the preferred party in the country by passing a Federal Election Act which provided financing, thus giving them special protection against outside challenges. So this combination of things, plus again Watergate and the cry of reform, came together and the Federal Election Act was passed. But it seems to me that the result of it is going to be a kind of homogenization of politics.

The third problem is the influence of television—particularly on campaigns—and the power of the networks to decide who the serious candidates are and how much exposure they are supposed to get. In this area there are supposed to be two protections in the law—one called "Equal Time," which says that if time is either sold or given to one candidate or to one party, the same amount has to be sold or given to the other party. And a broader rule called the "Fairness Doctrine," which says you can claim that your position has not been treated fairly.

In 1976 we challenged both of these rules promulgated by the Federal Communications Commission. And we lost on both of them, with the FCC and the courts sustaining the idea that if you had something like the League of Women Voters to give you cover, there was no limitation on the degree of discrimination that networks or television stations might exercise. Under this ruling the networks could refuse to sell the Libertarian candidate time because, he wanted it before the Republicans and Democrats had nominated their candidates, and they said this would give him an unfair advantage!

One night in 1976 we tried to buy a half hour, they said they could not sell it because it was "Maude's time." Now you may remember "Maude." "Maude" was a television show on Wednesday night at 8:00 p.m. And CBS, with one of their more original arguments, said that to sell this time to me would by the very act itself violate the equal time provisions of the law because no one else could ever buy that same time; that this was 30 minutes which was unique in the whole history of time. If they sold it to us and someone else came along and said, "We want Maude's time," they would have to say, "It is gone," and therefore under the rules they just could not sell it.

We could have gone to court I suppose, but we were in court about everything else so we let it pass. But the networks were using equal-time as an excuse to deny us TV time, although in the case of the Republicans and Democrats they were very careful to sell them equal time, or to give them equal time on news programs, even to the point of making sure that if Ford was on one night, Carter was on the next.

We did raise a case on the "fairness doctrine," in which we said we were not being given any general coverage apart from equal time. But again we lost when the court bought CBS's argument that I had been treated fairly because I had been mentioned or covered during seven and a half minutes in four months on their news programs—and two and a half minutes of that was on Walter Cronkite. If you are mentioned twice by Walter in four months you are supposed to be grateful; you have been kept alive. (We pointed out that in the same four months Walter had reported at length twice about an ape boy. Once he came on and said someone had discovered this boy raised by apes, and he was very excited by it. And about six weeks later Walter came on again and said they discovered that the boy was not raised by the apes, and he was just as enthusiastic. So we said, "Don't give us equal time with Ford and Carter, just treat us as well as you did the ape boy.")

This is a serious problem for candidates because if the networks decide not to cover you there's nothing you can do about it. Now I think you either have to try to enforce equal time and fairness or else—and I say this not just because of the problem of administering the law, but because of the nature of the influence of television—we probably ought to ban television political ads altogether.

Finally, let me say a word about the primary system. I think we have to get away from the present system because it does not work even though primaries continue to proliferate. In fact the more you get, the worse the system operates. My approach is to make it universal. Let us have a national primary because state by state primaries do not work. So let us have a national one.

I believe all of these things have to be attended to or the whole political process and the results of that process—our choice of national leaders—will continue to deteriorate.

CHISHOLM: My views on the presidential electoral process have to be taken in the context of certain facts. I am black and I am a woman and I dared in 1971-72 to go around this country to some 27 states and ask persons to give me their serious consideration to be the guardian of the Ship of State.

I learned a great deal in those 18 or 19 months that I ran around this country. I had an opportunity to speak with all kinds of persons and I have come to a certain number of conclusions on the basis of my experience and the stimuli to which I have been exposed, rather than on the basis of any academic, theoretical beliefs or approaches to this entire issue.

First of all, when we ask is the election process a good one or a bad one, we have to ask, good for whom? Good for what? Or bad for whom and bad for what? Because as with everything else in the United States of America those persons who usually participate in the process, become very involved, join a certain group or organization or fall in behind a certain kind of candidate, are for the most part the persons that do a great deal of reading, that keep abreast of the issues on a day-to-day basis, that have more than a day-today concern about life in general. They are not caught up with the question of survival. Whether or not they are going to be able to eat the next day or have a roof over their heads for a few months in the future?

What I am saying is that although this is presumably a representative democratic form of government, those who get caught up in the process are the people who do not have to feel some of the real negatives and the survival concerns that a large number of Americans do feel and therefore do not have the time or the patience to become involved with this entire process involving the election of a President.

I happen to think that the entire primary and caucus system in this country is for the birds. And that is the only way that I can really put it. We are supposed to be dealing with the question as to whether or not the American people—the people out there in the villages and the towns and the cities and the hills, just plain people on every level—are going to have some real input into the selection of an individual, be he a man or a woman or a black or a white with the necessary attributes or requisites for leadership in terms of trying to take this country down a certain path or trying to restore faith in what American democracy is supposed to be all about.

But one finds more and more that there is a kind of coalition of special interest groups, moneyed groups, the top level groups in this country that dominate this representative democratic process that so many persons in this nation are supposed to be involved in. In this whole business, the one thing that one cannot overlook constantly is money. Let us not talk about democracy. Let us not even talk about representative form of government. I am trying desperately not to be too cynical, but I am trying to put it exactly where it is at.

In our process money is the prime requisite. It has nothing to do with the potential or the real ability or talents or offerings of a man and/ or a woman who can give leadership to this country at any point in time. There is a great bearing on who you know, who has got some of the materials and the resources that are necessary if you are going to be able to try to run for such an office as president of this country. And when one addresses one-self to the caucuses and the primaries, for God's sake, let us stop kidding ourselves.

Caucuses are usually put together on the basis of the different candidates trying to get a lot of bodies out, even if the bodies do not understand what it is really all about. Even if the bodies have not had an opportunity to assess and evaluate, and really try to understand what is going on. The question is, which of the candidates will have access to the funds and the instrumentalities and mechanisms necessary for getting the bodies to a particular place at a particular time when the caucuses are going to be taking place. We cannot even discuss the ability or the powers or the aptitudes of the man or the woman who is seeking the support of the people, it does not extend to that level. I have participated in five conventions now. I have been very involved with the National Committeewoman of the Democratic party in New York. I have learned. I have watched and I have listened. And I am very, very cynical about the entire process. Very cynical, because I truly believe that the American people—and I am not talking about the privileged, the upper middle class and the upper class and those who have access to money and the inner circle—the mass of people do not really have the opportunity to become as involved as they should.

We realize that a lot of them do not become involved because they are concerned about survival on a day-to-day basis. But even beyond that, those who are in control and those who are reaching out do not pay too much attention to the masses out there. What is important to them is simply winning. They say to themselves, "I've got to win this office. I've got to be able to use every kind of situation at my command to be able to get control of the delegates necessary for me to come across." It has nothing to do with democracy.

The result is the cynicism and the disillusionment and the apathy and the constant diminution of the participation of the American people every four years in the political process that results in the election of a Chief of State for another four years. It is not alive and vital as it should be. And that is because, although people may not be able to enunciate it, they have come to feel that the process is not really for real; that they are not truly a part of it.

I think there are three things about the process that we have to look at. Number one, the media—the media just control everything. The media determine who is a bona fide candidate and who is not. The media determine those individuals to a large extent who are supposed to be in the forefront or who seem to be in the forefront. The media even get to the point where they really determine sometimes way in advance who they are going to kill off before there has been the opportunity to go out in the land and give oneself to the American people in terms of what one has to offer. The media sometimes cut that off even before the individual has that kind of an opportunity. The media are awesome. The media are powerful.

The media control. And God help you in this democratic land of ours if you are not a good person—whatever that word "good" means—in terms of being the traditional type of Republican or traditional type of Democrat, who does not rock the boat or question certain traditions that have been accepted down through the ages in this Republic.

If you do not fall into these categories, the media forget about you or try to kill you off as they did to Gene McCarthy and they did to me—because we were rejected by the power bosses, by those who make some determinations and then have their hook-ups with the media, the papers and the radio and the television. You are done before you get started.

Gene could not get but so far. He was doomed. And then you come down the line to a person such as myself. Just look at me, look at who I am. I am a black person. I am a female. Double jeopardy! And I wanted to go to the American people and have the American people make some assessments as to whether or not I possess certain requisites for leadership in this, my land, but how dare someone like me do that. So even before I got started, I was killed off. And killed off for a lot of other reasons—because I dared to be a very outspoken, assertive woman, a woman that had and continues to have tremendous confidence, and a woman that believes that I am just as good or better than most of these males running around.

Now even aside from the role of the media, when you go into the caucuses and the primaries, and you talk to the people, it is very strange. The most amazing thing that I have found about the people who come to a caucus being held in a given village or a given town is that 50 percent of them do not even know what is going on. They do not really understand what it is all about. It is wonderful for us to enunciate the notion that only America has a representative form of government where the people participate in the electoral process. But it is not the fact. So I believe the time has come in America when we should knock out the caucuses and the primaries as now practiced in this country for four basic reasons:

Number one, I think it is very unfair and I think it is physically, mentally, emotionally, psychologically exhausting on the part of a candidate to be going up the highways and the byways of this country for a period of anywhere from a year-and-a-half to two telling the American people, "Look at me. Give me a chance. This is my platform. This is what I'm running on." Number one, it's inhuman!

Number two, the people in our country justifiably or not get sick and tired of the politicians mouthing certain phrases, certain clichés every four years. You talk with the people and they will ask, "Look, so what's new? Candidates come out of the woodwork every four years telling us they have a dream. They promise us everything. We know full well that after it's all over this does not mean a hill of beans." So a longer campaign only leads to greater cynicism.

Three, I believe that the American people should be directly involved in the election of a president of this country. I do not want any electoral college; I do not want any transformations or interpretations or what have you when the people go to vote, they are casting their vote for the most important office in this country and they are casting their vote for that man or woman they believe should be guiding the ship of state for a period of four years. I believe in the direct election of the president.

Four, if indeed we have to continue the primary system, let us have a set of regional primaries. To have the candidates running around like chickens with their heads lopped off all over this country to participle in primaries is ridiculous. A candidate may move in one day from the deep South to the far North; then way out West. He or she never gets an opportunity to meditate, to know what he is really doing. The candidate never gets an opportunity to assess what is happening as he goes out in the highways and byways and he talks to the American people. He never gets a chance to come back and sit still and say, "Now what did I notice in that audience? What did the people seem to be perturbed or disturbed about?" No, because as soon as he gets done in one place he has to jump on another plane and go shooting off someplace else again. What madness is this?

And so you have people every four years running all over this country like they are crazy. You talk to them privately, the poor things can hardly stand up. but they have got to put that "front" up because it is important to put a front up. But I do not believe in putting fronts up, I believe in telling it like it is. And it is inhumane. So we should at least move in the direction of regional primaries, where maybe for one month or six weeks we will have the Eastern Seaboard conducting its primary so that the candidates can move from Connecticut to Delaware to New York to New Jersey because these states are near each other. We can each save some energy. We need energy. Then we could move to the South and have the Southern primaries. Maybe you can have two batches of primaries in the South because you have two distinct Southern divisions. You could have one batch in the Southeast, the other in the Southwest.

Regional primaries make sense, because if nothing else all the candidates can then concentrate on a given section of the country at a given time, conserve some of their energy, get a chance to pull themselves together and give the people a feeling that they are really spending some time with them.

The last point that I want to make has to do with the media. I have fought a great deal with the media. I know when I ran in '71 and '72, they made a determination that I was not important. And wherever I went, to the best of their ability they did not zero in on me. I will never forget that when I went to Florida over 700 people were at the airport, and of these 700 close to 650 were white people. And that was never mentioned by the media. I noticed during my campaign that there were so many things this country really needed to know about in terms of the democratic process but that these things were completely blocked out and blacked out. I often feared that the media were being controlled by certain forces in this country who did not want the people to begin to think that a black person who happens to be female could develop some kind of following.

But I wanted people to know that America is a multi-faceted, variegated country; that there are all kinds of people who make up America, and that you did not have to be white and you did not have to be male to be given consideration. I knew it would be hell, and I did catch hell, but I never regretted it for one moment.

WILSON: Senator McCarthy and Representative Chis-holm are disappointed office-seekers who have in common every ground for feeling that the presidential selection system did not treat them fairly. I think many of the particulars of their criticism of the system are accurate. The election laws, access to television and such, have often conspired in many real and important ways against persons who are not part of the political mainstream. And I think it is in large measure because of the efforts of Representative Chisholm and Senator McCarthy and George Wallace and others that some of these laws are being modified or reconsidered or at least that the issue is before us.

But by and large I do not agree with their analysis of the system. I certainly do not agree with Representative Chisholm in believing that the media control everything. I don't think that the money interests dominate. Indeed, quite the contrary. It is the computer-driven direct-mail advertising system that dominates, and it does not produce money for politics; it merely recycles it from persons who have it in small amounts to those who collect it in large amounts, and retain it in large amounts, yielding a small fraction for the candidates who have commissioned the direct mail.

I certainly do not think that a large number of the people or most of the people or all of the people are fooled by television advertisements or do not know what is going on. Indeed I have a somewhat sanguine view of human nature and the Democratic system.

Curiously enough however, though I do not accept the diagnosis, I arrive at many of the same conclusions; not in detail perhaps, but I certainly agree with the thrust of Representative Chisholm's remarks that the primary system demands the stamina of an athlete and the intelligence of a philosopher—and those two traits are not frequently combined as is evident to anyone such as myself who sat for a time on a Harvard College admissions committee. I think that one can reach these concerns and one can favor fairly profound changes in the present system from a different perspective: not what it is doing to the people, but what it is doing to the office of the Presidency.

The office of the Presidency, as I understand the founders when they wrote the Constitution, was created to achieve two main purposes. The first and most important purpose was to provide for the central management of foreign affairs on a day-to-day basis, subject to certain important powers given to the Senate, and to be the Commander in Chief of the Armed Services. That was without any doubt the single most important function the Chief Executive Officer was to have. Secondly, he was to have the function of being a check on the passions of a popular legislature by having a separate electoral base and the opportunity for presidential veto.

There may have been other concerns, but these two concerns dominated. And quite understandably, because at the time the Constitution was written the framers of the Constitution feared foreign invasion and foreign alliances, and bemoaned the inability of the separate confederated colonies to resist such foreign entry, and because they feared the possible tyranny of democratically elected legislatures and wished to see some check on temporary passions.

Now many years have passed since that document was written and one could reasonably argue that the important functions of the president have been enlarged, perhaps modified in some degree, but I would insist that the first of those functions, that is to say, the management of foreign affairs and the supervision of the military establishment remain the single most important responsibility to which each incumbent president in the last 30 or 40 years has turned his attention.

And I think that will continue in the future regardless of who occupies the office. Now if they are the most important functions—and I think it is something in the nature of nations that makes these functions necessarily devolve into some single pair of hands in each country—if they are the overriding functions, what has the presidential election system done? It seems to me that the proliferation of primaries, 36 in 1980, combined with the need to prepare for those primaries, has distracted the incumbents. It has meant that we really elect a president for only two years, during the first of which he learns the office, if we are fortunate; and during the second of which, perhaps if we are fortunate, he exercises the powers of that office. During the third and fourth years of his term he prepares for a re-election campaign.

I think it also creates powerful incentives for those who wish to challenge the president both from within the president's party or from other parties or from independent candidacies. It gives them an important incentive to spend two to four, or in the case of Governor Reagan, 12 years running for the Presidency, mobilizing the support sufficient to challenge an incumbent, precluding therefore any possibility of acquiring national administrative experience. The chief feature of the American directly-elected Presidency is that it brings to office persons who in modern times have had, in almost every case, no important national administrative experience.

For example, Herbert Hoover was the last American president to serve in a Cabinet. Some, such as Lyndon Johnson, have had some similar experience, many have had legislative experience which, though important, is not quite the same thing. I think that the demands placed on both the incumbent and the challengers by the protracted, expensive system of primary campaigns detracts importantly from the single most important function of the presidency. It may indeed detract from other of its functions but I am preoccupied with this one.

I conclude therefore that we should by some means reduce dramatically the number of primaries. Perhaps by having regional primaries; perhaps by having laws stipulating that primaries may not begin before a certain date or may not exceed a certain number. I do not propose to offer a specific plan, but I think the present system—in human as well as institutional terms—presents unacceptably high costs.

I think furthermore that the system offers too little opportunity for candidates to be tested by the judgment of their professional peers. I think the participation of elective office holders and party officials in the candidate selection process has diminished dramatically, and the participation of those whose principal interest is in the enthusiasms and charisma of individual candidates has risen dramatically. One of the characteristics of this latter group is that often they would rather be right than win, and I do not think the electorate as a whole is presented with satisfactory alternatives, if the alternatives are generated by groups of enthusiasts who would rather be right than president.

Even though one can imagine defects of any alternative system, I think the defects of the present system are quite clear. The timing and sequencing of the primaries means that a decision is often made prematurely. Jimmy Carter won the Democratic nomination for the presidency in 1976 literally within a few weeks after the New Hampshire primary when only a tiny fraction of the votes even in the Democratic primaries had been counted.

In 1980 we discovered that a former President of the United States, Gerald R. Ford, was in effect eliminated from serious consideration for the nomination for the presidency four months before the Republican convention was held. Now perhaps under a different system, Mr. Ford would still have been passed over. Under a different system, Mr. Carter might still have been nominated, though I think that unlikely. But I find it unfortunate not only that there are so many primaries spread over so many months, but that the sequencing of them so often builds a premature and un-examined commitment to a candidate who, for often transient strategic reasons, has managed to position himself in such a way with regard to the other candidates as to permit them to divide their constituency while a small minority attaches itself to what ultimately becomes the winning candidacy.

Finally, it seems to me that the effort to regulate this process by the Federal Government stands fair to deliver the entire presidential selection system into the hands of lawyers and accountants. Much of the money that goes to an election campaign at the presidential level and at the Congressional level is devoted to defensive actions designed to minimize the chances that one will fall afoul of the ever-changing rules of the Federal Election Commission, or that one will not by intent or by error commit a mistake that an opponent can seize upon during the event or after the event to discredit the other side.

The Federal Election Commission, like many regulatory commissions charged with overseeing a difficult part of our society's processes, has I think made a bad job worse by the proliferation of rules, by a tendency to change rules, and by a tendency to often put the most restrictive possible interpretations on those rules. I am not sure that any system of federally funded elections can be totally immune to this, but surely we can divorce the process of financing elections from the bureaucratic rigor mortis that has set in the Federal Election Commission, which I think exacerbates all of the qualities I just described.

The present system tends to reward candidates who can take an early lead in the primaries, because if they spend all their money early and they have made the right strategic decision, they can coast home spending relatively little money. Others, who decide to spend later, may find themselves ruled out of the competition before the money is spent or the votes are counted. And I think the tendency to insist that the money be collected in very small amounts—amounts that given the current levels of inflation are ludicrously small—means that those who now raise money from the public for presidential election campaigns are raising it by a kind of appeal which is designed to or has the effect of exacerbating the hostilities of the electorate. For unfortunately the most effective appeal you can make to a person who may give you $25.00 a year is an appeal that awakens in the man or woman the deepest, most morbid suspicions and concerns about politics. So the system feeds public cynicism and distrust. It brings to the fore, groups of a special-interest or a single-issue nature which have small, but intense and impassioned, followings. And I think that this leads candidates to cultivate that part of the electorate which though important in the primaries is of the least importance in the general election.

As a result, when the candidates selected by this process appear before the general electorate, it is hardly surprising to discover that the general electorate finds so little in them inspiring. The people find that the candidates do not somehow represent them. Especially since the candidates, having gone through this system of appealing to intense minorities for the purpose of raising money, must now broaden their appeal to attract more votes. This rather dramatic change in tone and posture and often in explicit policy positions does not pass unnoticed, since I for one do not think the American voters are dopes. I think by and large they are relatively well informed on the general policy dispositions of candidates, if not on their detailed proposals. I do not think that candidates are sold to them by television the way bars of soap are presumably sold. I do think, however, that they notice that the system induces disingenuity among the candidates, and induces in them a kind of inconsistency which voters find dismaying: namely, a tendency to over-promise and under-produce, to appeal to the darkest rather than the brightest side of human nature as a way of justifying an appeal that sets the individual candidate apart from the pack.

The best way to survive the primary process, it seems to me, is to say that you are unlike all of your rivals in some one important respect. All of the rivals represent the "establishment" or the "system" or the Democrats or the Republicans or whatever, and you are different. And to make that a credible strategic position, you then have to criticize all others in rather global terms. Therefore candidates running for office increasingly claim that the system is not working, that it is bad, that our government is not functioning properly, and that the best evidence is this collection of turkeys who happen to be my opponents.

In short, the primary election system, rather than inducing individuals to build coalitions, induces individuals to separate themselves from their rivals, and that it seems to me does not help the problem of building popular confidence in government.

BRAMS: I have three specific proposals to make. My perspective is to try and look at the rules of the game and use models—mathematical models—specifically game theory, to draw out the implications of these rules and then try to say how they might be improved upon to make them more equitable, more fair for the candidates.

Let me start with the primary process. Being from New Hampshire, I am a bit chauvinistic about keeping New Hampshire first among the primary states. I think New Hampshire in a sense saved Eugene McCarthy in 1968 when he got 42 percent of the vote—and became the darling of the media—against Lyndon Johnson who got 50 percent. So I don't think Senator McCarthy can complain on the basis of his first try. And the fact that he was about to win in the Wisconsin primary a month later induced Lyndon Johnson to withdraw the night before.

The primary process allows unknowns to come from nowhere. Jimmy Carter is another example. And I think that is good. But I think that can only be sustained by starting in a small state like New Hampshire or perhaps Iowa. I think regional primaries are going to hurt the unknowns, and I think a national primary is going to all but rule them out. Of course the process has to start somewhere, so why not in a small state? Although I would agree that 36 or 38 primaries can be very difficult on the candidate, nevertheless this is a matter of popular choice. This is popular choice on the part of potentially 80 percent of the voters in the United States, with respect to the nomination of a candidate for their party.

The problem with primaries is that some voters in some states have undue influence. New Hampshire is an example. Iowa is also. Conversely, many Californians may not have voted in 1980 because they had no influence on the nominations of either the Democratic or Republican candidates despite the fact that California has almost 10 percent of the population of the United States.

To remedy this defect, I would propose to depreciate the votes of the primaries that come first. Thus all primary states voting before say March 1st in a Presidential election year would have their votes, their delegate votes, depreciated by say 75 percent. That would include New Hampshire as the first primary state usually voting at the end of February.

Those voting in March might be depreciated 50 percent; those in April, 25 percent; those in May or later would get full credit. Thereby the undue influence, if you will, of the first primary or caucus states would be depreciated, and although there would still be a lot of media tension in the first states, there would not be that many votes. I think this would be one way of equalizing the process. You see, even going to regional primaries, they would have to start somewhere, in New England or the South, and that would give undue influence to that particular region. So I think this kind of weighted voting system would be one way to deal with the problem.

The second problem is the electoral college. Now mountains have been written about the electoral college. Let me only point out that if one measures the power of a voter by his ability to change the outcome of an election by changing his vote, then a voter in California has approximately three times the power of a voter in Alaska or another small state with only three electoral votes. That seems to be a manifest violation of the one person-one vote Supreme Court decision. The fact is that voters in large states count for three times as much as the voters in small states, because of the unit rule feature of the electoral college, which gives all the electoral votes of a state to the plurality winner.

Accordingly, by changing my vote in California I can potentially affect a huge block of votes which could change the outcome much more probably than changing the outcome by changing my vote in Alaska. The unit rule feature has a very biased effect in favor of the largest state. The fact that we now largely have one person-one vote with respect to the House since the reapportionment decisions beginning in 1962, gives us an argument that we need balance in the whole system.

I think we should have one person-one vote in presidential elections, which means direct popular vote rather than a strange institution like the electoral college. Incidentally, the electoral college unit rule feature is not written into the Constitution. It is a custom that states cast all their votes for the plurality winner. So one does not need a Constitutional amendment to change that feature.

My third recommendation is for "approval voting" in elections at all the levels. Approval voting is an election system in which the voter can vote for as many candidates as he likes in a multi-candidate election. Thus, if there were five candidates, you would not be restricted to voting for just one candidate. You could vote for two, three, four or even five, although your vote in that case would not make any difference.

The advantage here is that it allows voters to do everything they can under the present system. Vote for their favorite, if they have a favorite. But if they do not have a favorite they can indicate that fact by voting for more than one, showing that more than one is acceptable. And in the early primaries which typically attract fields of candidates of five to ten, it seems to me that voters have great difficulty and should be allowed this greater flexibility of choice.

For example, if you were a liberal Democrat in New Hampshire in 1976, you probably would have had a pretty tough choice among the three liberals starting out in the Democratic primary race. But you could have expressed that liberal point of view under approval voting by voting for all three. This is not a ranking system; it is a system in which the candidate with the most approval votes wins. And it would tend to favor the strongest candidate, the candidate most acceptable, the candidate most approved of by the most voters.

It elects the strongest candidate, instead of a George McGovern who in 1972 won the Democratic primaries with only about 25 percent of the total primary vote, or a Barry Goldwater in 1964 who also was a minority candidate. I think other candidates might have won in those election years if there had been approval voting. I would argue it is best for the parties because it prevents nominating disastrous candidates like Goldwater or McGovern, who then give the voters no viable choice in the general election because they are foregone losers.

But it also gives minority candidates their proper due. George Wallace in 1968 got 13.5 percent of the total popular vote. Under approval voting,—according to some computer simulations—he probably would have gotten about 22 percent of the vote, because voters would not have drifted away from him thinking he had no chance. Similarly, Eugene McCarthy in 1976 was showing 5 to 7 percent in the popular polls but got only .9 percent of the popular vote on election day. I think the fact that one in 20 voters favored Eugene McCarthy in '76 should have been registered, and minority candidates, even if they cannot win, would get their proper due under approval voting.

The number of candidates is also better accounted for. If a new candidate enters, you do not necessarily have to take your vote away from somebody else in order to vote for him. I think it could increase voter turnout because voters who find several candidates acceptable but cannot make a choice would be more likely to go to the polls.

Approval voting is superior to preferential voting for a number of technical reasons. Practically it can be implemented on existing voting machines. To go into effect, approval voting would require only a change in election law, not a general Constitutional change. For example, the election law in New Hampshire with respect to presidential primaries would only have to be amended as follows: "Every qualified voter shall have an opportunity to vote his preference [preferences] on the ballot of his party for his choice [choices] of one person [any persons] to be the candidate [candidates] of his political party for President of the United States." It requires only statutory change not Constitutional change, and could be readily implemented.

Approval voting, direct election of the president, and depreciation of votes in the early primaries to prevent undue influence and premature decisions—these are my three suggestions for improving the presidential selection process.

Questions and Comments on the Selection/Election Process

What are the vital factors—ideology, money, television—in winning election today?

Not ideology, and particularly not at the presidential level. Our politics is not really programmatic, and the main reason is the need to satisfy a very diverse electorate, which requires candidates—certainly national candidates—to adopt centrist positions.

People often ask, how is it possible that the Democrats have had control of the Congress for fifty years (with the exception of two very brief times in 1946 and 1952) and at the same time the presidential elections have divided evenly, four and four? Well the answer is that you can run as a Democrat for Congress in New York and as a Democrat for Congress in Mississippi on entirely different programs and be elected, because you are only responsible to your own local constituency. But nationally as a presidential candidate you cannot say a different thing in Mississippi than you say in New York because it is going to be on television or in the papers and they are going to trip you up. That is why Reagan has moved toward the center with the speed of light. Anderson has done the same thing. Carter has always been there in the middle, and the other two candidates are trying to elbow him out of the way. Because if you get too far off the center, you are going to lose, and you are going to lose because you are going to make more enemies than you make friends. You are going to lose because 40% of the people may be for you but 60% are against. It is as simple as that. To win, where there is no proportional representation system, where if you get 5% of the vote you get 5% of the seats in Parliament, candidates have got to appeal to the broad middle of the electorate.

So the conclusion is that if you are running for office in America, you need five things: You need a good candidate, you need a good issue, you need a good organization, you need good money, and above all else, you need good luck Now if you have got all five of these, you are a cinch, an^[1] if you have not got any of them you are going to lose, the problem is suppose you have got 2.4 of these five characteristics, then what?

The hardest factor to deal with of course is luck. For example, say a candidate happens to be campaigning on a "no-news day," and he says or does something that would not ordinarily hit the news but on such a day it does. Several years ago there was a New York election for the Senate which ultimately came down to Pat Moynihan and Bella Abzug. One day Bella was asked whether she would support the Democratic candidate and she said she was not sure.

That is what she had been saying all along. It was no news. But it went out on the wires on a no-news day, it hit the headlines, and it had a major impact on the election. There is also the converse situation, of course, where on a big news day, things that would otherwise hit the news, do not hit the news.

In any event, a candidate can only hope and pray that if he is going to make a "boo-boo," it will be on a big-news day when it will be hidden on page 20 where nobody will see it.

Television and money are very important but they are not the end-all and be-all of American politics. For example, John Connally in seeking the Republican nomination in 1980 raised more money than anybody else-except possibly Reagan—and he ended up with one Convention delegate. Conversely, John Anderson had almost no money, and he ran for president with a possibility of winning. Furthermore, in 1978 there were eight candidates for the Congress who spent more than half a million dollars each. Six lost; only two won.

Are we heading toward a system in which the media consultant is more important than the candidate himself?

In a campaign the media consultant is already more important than the candidate. But he can also be more important both before and after the campaign itself. For example: In 1977 there were about six people who wanted to run for Mayor of New York City, all of them out of their minds. And I listened to what they were saying about six months and not one of them I thought was saying anything that made any sense at all in terms of the needs of the city. And I started putting together articles and speeches and proposals to deal with the problems we faced, which I sent to them. I did not get any response at all from any of those candidates, and none of them echoed anything I had said. So I decided I would run myself and I would force them to face up to such nonsense as saying we must increase the police force when in fact there is no money to increase the police force and you are going to have to reduce the police force.

One of the people whom I had particularly been leaning on was Ed Koch. And for six months he had called and I had sent him stuff. I had never gotten a response. I listened to what he said in public, and he did not seem to have heard anything. But David Garth read the material that I had written, and one day Koch called me and said I would like to meet with you.

I met with Garth and him, and Garth said I have read all the stuff you have written and you are absolutely right and I have tested it out and this is going to be our campaign. I looked at him and I said that is swell David, that is your campaign, but what about Koch? He has been listening to this for eight months, and I have not heard a word out of him. How do I know that he is really going to go to bat on these issues? And Garth's response was a classic. He said, to prove my good faith I have already stolen two of them. And indeed he had. From that point on Koch faithfully adhered to every one of those positions. Now why? Because Garth had the wit to understand that what was being said was what was needed to be said and that you could win on it.

Now let me take it a step further. That is the campaign side and I think it is true of almost every campaigner since McGovern. He did not listen to his media people, and he was a disaster on account of it. But I am sure that Carter and Ford and Reagan and all the rest of them are doing what everybody else does. Here is where it gets dangerous, because it carries over once they get elected. A professor at the University of Chicago did an article in which he analyzed Carter's August 1979 speech on energy and compared it to the poll that was taken by Pat Cadell two weeks before. It is perfectly clear that that speech was written on the basis of that poll, even though the questions were misleading as hell. I know that in 1979 when Koch fired all of his Deputy Mayors in New York City he did it in response to a poll. Now the media people are aware of this and there is nothing more attractive to somebody who manages a campaign than to have the power to run the government afterwards. So there is a real danger of having governmental policy decisions made not on the basis of any long-term view as to where a government ought to be going but upon the results of a poll taken by a good pollster or sometimes not such a good pollster.

One exception to this that I can think of is a decision made by the Governor of New York. Governor Carey was running for reelection in 1978. He was in dreadful trouble. He was a great Governor in a crisis and in between he liked not to govern too much. He had made a lot of enemies and his pollster—the same Mr. Garth—told him as everybody else did, Governor you have got to be for capital punishment. Koch was for capital punishment and it helped him, and every poll said that the people wanted a return to capital punishment for certain crimes. It was about two to one in terms of popular response. But Carey said, "No I am not for capital punishment. I think it is a bad thing for a government to do. Not only will I not support it, but if capital punishment is passed I will reprieve every prisoner who is condemned to death." That is a pretty gutsy thing to do. Especially when you are running for reelection and you know two thirds of the people are against you. But he won. Now that is unusual. But it demonstrates that there are public officials who still say, Hey wait a minute, I am running a government; I am not running a popularity contest. I hope we start electing people that have that kind of vision as to where they are going, but the hope that we are going to end up with someone who has a sense of what government is all about seems to be more and more remote, and it scares the hell out of me.

Does the federal election financing legislation need revision?

I think the big reform we need is to take a lot of the money out of the process. I see that happening in several ways.

One is that I think ultimately we are going to go to a single primary one day in the spring of the election year throughout the country instead of the current series of multiple primaries which are extremely costly. The reason I think that is going to happen is because the television networks cannot afford to cover this string of primaries and they will get interested in the idea that if we just had one, say on April 21, and elected the delegates we would not have to have the crews running around the country at tremendous cost.

If that happens the next step will be that the convention will be a lot more significant because the candidates will come out of that one primary and somebody will have 33%, somebody will have 22% and somebody will have 18%, and the convention will once again become a significant deliberative body as the delegates seek to decide who among all these people is the best. But that will take a lot of money out of the process because candidates are not going to have to run from state to state to state to state.

The second elimination of funds that I think is going to be inevitable is a cut in the cost of television advertising by guaranteeing a degree of free exposure. We should face up to the reality that 90% of the money raised for a political campaign is spent on electronic media—the television and radio stations—all of which are given a massive free gift by the people of the United States from whom they get their franchise. ABC, CBS, NBC pay about $500 a year or something to get the right to their channels in New York City, and it would seem only proper that part of the price they should pay for the privilege of monopolizing our airways is to provide free time for political candidates. I think the Federal Election Commission will be the one that ends up allocating free television time and enforcing it, not the Federal Communications Commission, which is owned by the networks although they are supposed to be regulated by it.

The third step that I see is to limit the period during which candidates can spend money. By that I mean the period prior to the national primary is an appropriate time to expose the public to the virtues and defects of the candidates. After that the need for advertising on television will diminish until the convention is over.

The campaign now starts the day after the convention is over. That did not used to be true. Traditionally the campaign used to start on Labor Day, and eight weeks was regarded as plenty of time for a national campaign. It makes an awful lot of sense to hold off for a bit and then go ahead and do anything you want to do for eight weeks. We should make such restraint a condition for whatever federal financing there would be.

Thus there would continue to be federal financing but on a much lower level because the major federal contribution would be to make available the free electronic media time.

Such time should also be spread around a little. There are congressional candidates and senatorial candidates who cannot get anywhere near television, and they should get a cut out of that free time. Ultimately state candidates should also share it. The Federal Election Commission could set aside a portion of the time that networks and licensed stations have in each state, and let the state do the allocation. That is the direction which I see election financing reform taking, and I hope it will because I think it might give us a little bit more rational a process.

What is the significance of single-interest groups in American politics?

In our modern complex society, democracy and free speech come from the check you send to your interest group. The individual really does not have any more influence in a society of nearly 250 million people.

So, many people find the expression of their free speech in the check that they send to this kind of organization. It may be pro- or anti-abortion, it may be pro- or anti-gun control, it may be ideological, it may be a very narrowly based interest like the cotton producers association, or the slate makers union, or it may be business or labor or somebody else, Evangelicals for example.

They hope the organization will represent their views. If they have strong ideological views, they can join a left wing pressure group like the Americans for Democratic Action, or a right wing pressure group like Americans for Constitutional Action, or they may have a particular thing they are interested in and join or form an organization for just that interest.

In the late 19th century there were two major single-interest groups in America, which make the contemporary pressure groups look very insignificant, and those two were women's suffrage and the prohibition movement. These people, the suffragettes, for example did not care whether a candidate was Republican or

Democrat, left or right, wet or dry. All they cared about was: are you right on suffrage—and if you were right on suffrage, you got the vote. (What was intriguing of course, was that it was men who voted women's suffrage, although women were also persuaded of rectitude eventually.) The prohibition movement was so strong that in the '20s you used to have in Congress a caucus called the Wet-Dry caucus. Now the Wet-Dry caucus consisted of members who drank wet and voted dry. And the Anti-Saloon League could not have cared less, you could stagger onto the floor, blind drunk, as long as you cast your vote dry.

All of this is all right as long as these interest groups are free to operate in an uninhibited way. I think it is one of the more effective ways in which the little man, the average citizen, gets to have some clout in this society. He or she is convinced that in an electorate as big as ours his own vote really does not make that much difference and he has not got time to start canvassing his street and saying I am for such and such. So it is probably the political action groups that represent, in a very real way, the active refuge of the free speech advocates.

Does the primary system need reforming—and if it does what kinds of changes should be made?

The direct primary system is based on the principle that the cure for the ills of democracy is more democracy. I dissent from that proposition. I think democracy is a means to achieve certain objectives of which justice and liberty and tranquility are among the most important.

I would only suggest modestly that it would be useful if the primaries were sufficiently reduced in importance so that when the convention took place, there would be a healthy fraction of office holders, both elected and party officials, who would participate. It should be a sufficiently large fraction so that no one could win, nail down the nomination, with just the primary vote. He would, after having tested himself or herself in the primary, still have to go to a convention where it is possible that his candidacy could be rejected. This would give him an incentive to negotiate with all of the elements in society, which is appropriate since he wants to represent so many different regions and ethnic and other groups that the need to build a coalition should manifestly be required of anyone no matter how successful they were in a primary.

Usually in states that have primaries for Congressional offices or for Governor and so on, the party meets first and picks the candidate they recommend. We should do that with the presidency too. Then in the primary voters can say, "We reject the party's nominee." We do not do this in the presidential primary now and it is ridiculous. We do it the other way. We let the public make a choice and then the party meets and tries to reverse the public, which is utterly irrational and contrary to the representative process.

The second thing which I think is undesirable is that in many primaries the candidate's name is not on the ballot. When I ran for President in 1968 my name was not on the ballot, so I could not win. I had to run delegates who had to go out to the people and say, "Look, I am running for McCarthy." This is basically the idea that was inherent in the Electoral College process—that responsible people would go to the voters, be chosen, and then go to a meeting and make a decision. I would like to see this adopted. To have the person go out and say, "Look, this is what I stand for. I represent candidate X." Then the voters choose and then the winners go to a convention and make their decision.

Moreover, I would like to see the Electoral College run on about the same basis. I would like to see the country with maybe 2500 presidential electoral districts where you could go out and compete, and you would elect 2500 people by whatever process, and they would go to a convention and pick a president. This would be a return to constitutional principles and representative government.

In a multi-faceted, variegated society such as the United States of America there is a tendency to have in contrast to other nations of the world, a much more broad, pluralistic kind of society. A much more variegated grouping of people from all parts of the world assembled in this country which is not really a melting pot but a solid bowl. So one has to be constantly about the business of trying to find ways of improving the system to be reflective of the democratic experience.

We have been making some changes recently on the national level within the past ten years as a result of pressures and challenges by minority candidates. And I dare say that in the future we are going to be seeing other changes. But my hope is that I will live to see the direct election of the President of the United States of America.

We suffer mostly because we let Rousseau affect the founding fathers more than Locke. So we can blame it on the French. What we do in a direct election is say that nothing should intervene between the voter and his decision. No person, no real challenge other than his own particular judgment. The projection of this idea is direct primaries, have the people making a decision in a kind of absolute no-intervention, no-intermediate stage.

I am for representative government. It carries us a stage beyond DeTocqueville and his worry about the tyranny of the majority over the minority. We are now moving into a stage where the majority in this country has begun to tyrannize itself. And that is the ultimate perversion of democracy.

Should there be a national primary?

A national primary is supported by most of the voters in public opinion polls but it would be an utter disaster because it undercuts so many other values. Democracy involves more than casting a ballot. It certainly involves discussion and the consideration of alternatives.

A national primary presumably would be held on a single day throughout the country and that would be it, whereas the present system at least gives you some opportunity to see how things develop, how a person does in different places, and how he reacts under pressure, and so on. A national primary would all be over in one day. There would be no opportunity for the development of trends.

In addition there are technical problems. Presuming there will be more than two candidates in most cases, a national primary might well be won by somebody like Jimmy Carter in New Hampshire with 28% of the vote. Is that a legitimate democratic choice? We could have runoffs. But there are problems with that. The leader in the national primary would probably be the candidate who starts out with the most money and/or with the most television attention. There would be no opportunity for somebody to come from a relatively obscure position; people like Carter, McGovern and Anderson would be totally eliminated. So it would have this terrible effect of limiting choice. It seems to be the most democratic thing you can do, but it would really limit the choice of the electorate.

I would make the plea for increased party participation. I think party politicians are about as bright as most people on average. They are self-interested of course but that is all right. What they are self-interested in is getting a candidate who can win and who can deal with people, and that is what a president ought to be.

Sol would be in favor of vastly increasing the number of party officials who go to a convention without being chosen in a primary, who go ex-officio—simply by virtue of their office. I would also have every member of Congress from that party automatically be a delegate. I would have every Governor who is in that party automatically be a delegate. I would have the Mayors of the 50 largest cities who are in that party automatically be delegates. And a sample of state legislators too. Indeed I would not be unhappy if as much as 50% of that convention were made up of party officials.

Then we would also have the evidence of the primaries. The voters would have a chance to say what they want. The candidates could still go around trying to prove what they can do. But they would also have to prove themselves to party officials.

Is the two-party system working?

I think we should note that the conception of government under the Constitution was one which included some thought that we would not have the instability that you can get from a multi-party parliamentary system. But also the men who drafted the Constitution said that the worst thing you could have would be two-party politics. John Adams said the worst thing was to have the politics of the country controlled by two political factions. But we have got the two factions now.

We do not have the instability of a multi-party parliamentary system. But once we are committed, we are sort of stuck. I mean at least in a parliamentary system you can bring down a government, we cannot do that except on two counts: constitutionally you can impeach a president for high crimes and misdemeanors or you can throw him out because he is insane. But you cannot do anything about stupidity. And so there is a whole range of misgovernment which goes untouched, except every four years. They say the two party system works, you know, even the academics say that. Then you take a look at it and you say. "Well what has it produced?" Then it gets pretty rough when you have to say,

"Well, we went from George Washington to Richard Nixon and from John Adams to Spiro Agnew."

The structure of our political system is biased in favor of two parties, two candidates. But it seems to me that system is in trouble now. A number of political leaders are bemoaning the fact that the party function seems to have withered away and that we now have significant third party candidates like Eugene McCarthy or George Wallace, indicating that the two-party system is in trouble. I think the system is dying, and that is why I recommend something like approval voting. Approval voting would tell us in a true sense whether Anderson is more acceptable than either of the other two candidates. If Carter Democrats worrying about Reagan on the right can also vote for Anderson because he is more acceptable than Reagan, and if Reagan Republicans worrying about Carter on the left, can also vote for Anderson because he is more acceptable than Carter, then Anderson would truly be the consensus candidate in the middle. He would be elected and in my opinion should be elected because this is the expression of popular choice.

Meanwhile, however, I expect that the parties will continue to get weaker, that primaries and caucuses will become more typical, that federal control over election money and federal rules over parties will become more intense, that the electoral college will in one way or the other be disbanded in favor of either direct election or the proportional split of votes, and that all of these things taken separately will be approved of by the voters. But they will notice at the end of the process that they are still profoundly dissatisfied with the results.